Games & Activities for
Primary Modern Foreign Languages

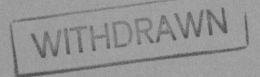

Other titles in the series

Barron: *Practical ideas, games and activities for the primary classroom*

Games & Activities
for
Primary Modern Foreign Languages

Nicola Drinkwater

PEARSON

Longman

Harlow, England • London • New York • Boston • San Francisco • Toronto
Sydney • Tokyo • Singapore • Hong Kong • Seoul • Taipei • New Delhi
Cape Town • Madrid • Mexico City • Amsterdam • Munich • Paris • Milan

Edinburgh Gate
Harlow CM20 2JE
United Kingdom
Tel: +44 (0)1279 623623
Fax: +44 (0)1279 431059
website: www.pearsoned.co.uk

First edition published in Great Britain in 2008

ISBN: 978-1-4058-7392-5

British Library Cataloguing in Publication Data
A CIP catalogue record for this book can be obtained from the British Library

Library of Congress Cataloging in Publication Data

Drinkwater, Nicola.
   Games & activities for primary modern foreign languages / Nicola Drinkwater
         p. cm
   Includes bibliographical references and index.
   ISBN 978-1-4058-7392-5 (alk. paper)
   1. Languages, Modern--Study and teaching (Elementary)--Activity
programs. I. Title. II. Title: Games and activities for primary modern
foreign languages.
   LB1578. D75 2008
   372.65--dc22   2008018977

10 9 8 7 6 5 4 3
12

Set by 30
Printed and bound in Great Britain by Henry Ling Limited, at the Dorset Press, Dorchester, DT1 1HD

Contents

Exploring literacy in the target language   185

Enhancing the language-learning experience   207

Part 3
Vocabulary lists   255

French   256

Introduction

The activities in this book are those I have used in my lunchtime and after-school clubs held at primary schools in my local area, and also in lessons I have been asked by headteachers to provide as part of the school curriculum. This book is aimed at all those delivering modern foreign languages (MFL) at Primary level to children from Reception (or even pre-school) onwards, whether specialist or non-specialist – these may include teachers, language specialists, foreign language assistants and teaching assistants. The activities you will find here range from 5-minute gap-fillers and short games to activities that can take up an entire lesson and projects that span several lessons. Although I have not used a course book myself and simply use activities like these to introduce young learners to MFL, nonetheless the activities found in this book can all be used to supplement a primary language-learning course book if you or your school/nursery has chosen to use one. Also, while I have personally used these games and activities to introduce children to French, German and Spanish – and therefore these are the only languages referred to in the book – the content is mostly non-language specific and can be used to teach and practise whichever language, or languages, you or your school have chosen to introduce.

Why is there a need for this book?

This book is not intended as a syllabus and nor can it claim to deliver all the aims and objectives of the Key Stage 2 Framework for Languages, as outlined in the QCA Schemes of Work (see www.qca.org.uk/mflschemes). There is already a wide range of course books available for teaching primary MFL, which tend to be language-specific. There is also a huge range of software for interactive whiteboards, CDRoms, bilingual books, classroom display materials, language-learning games and endless downloadable material on the internet (some of it doubtless better quality than the rest). There is a place for all of these in the primary MFL classroom.

The Key Stage 2 Framework groups the learning objectives for each unit into those concerned with literacy, oracy and intercultural understanding. You will find the contents of this book offer opportunities to develop all three of these areas; some activities involve two or all three at once. The emphasis, however, is mainly on oral skills and it is my own experience (and, I believe, that of others) that of the three sets of learning objectives it is the most difficult to find teaching materials that target oracy skills.

The recently published *Teacher's Guide – Languages: A scheme of work for Key stage 2* (Qualifications and Curriculum Authority 2007, visit www.qca.org.uk to order a copy) makes it clear that the 'use of games and activities requiring a physical response' has a valid presence as one of a range of teaching approaches. It advocates the use of 'a variety of visual aids' as well as 'active learning and the use of different senses'. The guide recognises that 'the use of enjoyable activities, including games, rhymes and songs, will enable children to repeat new language in a motivating way' and suggests a number of such games teachers might like to try. In general, the physical activity/games approach is endorsed as a way of enabling children to develop 'a positive attitude towards language learning', one of the Government's quoted key aims of introducing MFL into the primary curriculum.

I wholeheartedly agree with this aim and my intention is that this book will help teachers to achieve just that. In fact I would go further, and say that without physical expression through role-play, fun and game-playing during the early stages of their language-learning journey we risk putting children off for life. This is really the underlying philosophy here – give as many of these games and activities as possible a try and you'll probably find, as I have, that some will work with your group while others won't; sometimes you will know why and sometimes you won't, but I promise you that on the whole the children will have fun and enjoy the challenge of 'playing' with language – and surely that is what it's all about.

What will I need?

Using props wherever possible will fire the imagination and help children remember connections between words and objects, especially the very young who love to touch and hold things while they are learning their names. Flashcards are all very well but if you are teaching foods, why not bring in some real or plastic fruit and vegetables? Or a little toy car, plane and boat if you are teaching vehicles? Most children love to dress up and you can get a lot of mileage out of a pair of flip-flops, an old overcoat and a hat if you are teaching different types of weather. If, like me, you are on a budget and are fond of visiting charity shops, look out for simple educational jigsaws or boardgames – you can often place home-made stickers with target language (TL) words over the English words and create a new classroom resource.

A few items that I have found invaluable to have constantly on hand are:

- badges with TL names on
- dice
- playing cards
- A4 coloured paper/card
- CD player with CDs of children's songs in the target language
- set of plastic foods
- boxes, bags and containers
- beanbags

- a scarf to use as a blindfold
- a few tennis or other small balls.

Make up actions to help children remember new vocabulary that cannot easily be represented with props – sports, the weather, the seasons … can all be enacted with a simple physical gesture that helps to lodge the new language in the children's minds.

Young children will love it if you bring in a puppet or doll and tell them he or she only speaks the target language. Don't forget to give the doll a TL name (my two dolls who only speak French and German respectively are called Pipi and Caca! No, I haven't told the children what the names mean …). The children will be delighted when their questions in the target language elicit a response from the doll and find it hilarious if they try to ask something in English only to find he/she doesn't understand. The doll can join in with games and songs, encouraging the children to use new words and phrases. It's an important step towards grasping why they are learning a foreign language at all – sometimes the communicative purpose of speaking a foreign language can get lost in the haze of learning strange new sounds, seemingly for their own sake. Creating situations that mimic real life enables children to see this communicative purpose more clearly.

I strongly recommend you get hold of a CD of children's songs in your chosen target language – you can play it in the background while the children are involved in a game or activity, learn the words and sing the songs together, perform them in class assembly … It is well documented that new language content is much easier to learn and remember when set to music. You could buy such a CD next time you are abroad, ask a friend or colleague who is going on holiday to bring one back, or purchase one via the internet.

Finally, the more you use this book the clearer it will become to you that, with a little imagination, almost any children's game, song, rhyme, story or activity can be adapted to present some new foreign language content, or to practise what has already been learnt. Think of the party games you played as a child, or the activities you have done with your own children – which of these could be used to teach some new vocabulary?

How do I use this book?

The games and activities included in this book are divided into five sections:

- *Practising numbers and counting*. Learning to count and develop number skills in a foreign language is an on-going process which needs constant recapping and as a teacher you will probably find you need to return to this area more frequently than any other. The range of games here will hopefully furnish you with lots of different ways to practise counting, pronunciation, simple maths and monetary usage.

* *Practising specific vocabulary areas.* When you wish to concentrate on core vocabulary this section offers lots of ideas for learning and practising a particular topic area. However, I cannot claim to have covered all the main topic areas outlined in the QCA Schemes of Work here, and you will probably find some activities in this book that introduce vocabulary not included in the National Curriculum.
* *Practising vocabulary on many different topics.* These offer lots of fun and flexible ways of practising any vocabulary topic on which you happen to be focusing. Some will lend themselves more to certain themes than others, but if you approach this section with an open mind you will find the children in your class will develop favourite games, to which you can then return again and again.
* *Improving literacy in the target language.* While most of the rest of the book contains activities aimed at developing oral skills, this section is full of great ideas that involve reading and/or writing.
* *Enhancing the language-learning experience.* The activities in this section are 'nice-to-have' add-ons, if you like. Some of them require more planning, preparation and resources than an average lesson but will give the children something really special to remember. Others simply didn't seem to fit into any of the other categories above, or otherwise involve 'specialist' vocabulary, or simply involve the children playing and using new language elements for their own sake.

The links to other subjects do not refer to any specific units as outlined in the National Curriculum; they are merely my own suggestions. However, the QCA *Teacher's Guide* gives details of how the National Framework for Languages can enhance children's learning in many other curriculum subjects, including literacy, maths, science, geography, music and PE.

The learning objectives met by each individual activity are listed throughout the book; these refer to the learning objectives as outlined in the Key Stage 2 Framework for Languages. I have included a full list of these learning objectives for Years 3–6 in table form for easy reference (see pages 4–11). However, just because a game covers, say, three of the Year 4 learning objectives, this does not mean it cannot be useful to, and enjoyed by, children who are older or younger. It very much depends on the range of ability of your group and what, or how much (if any), language learning experience they have previously had.

The book also includes a vocabulary section for each of the three languages I teach, and which I assume will be most widely taught in primary schools – French, German and Spanish. This will be crucial for non-specialists, to avoid spending hours looking up key vocabulary in a dictionary, and will hopefully provide a useful reminder/checklist for those who already know the languages well. It may also prove a useful starting point for collating relevant vocabulary if you wish to use these activities to teach a further language not included here, which I hope many of you will feel inspired to do.

However, throughout the book wherever I have cited a word or phrase used during an activity in the target language, I have exclusively used French – this is because I think it likely that more primary MFL teachers will have a command of French in common than either of the other two languages. Apologies to Spanish and German speakers, who I hope will not feel excluded!

At the back of the book I have included sections on 'World festivals' and 'Birthdays around the world' to provide a starting point for some opportunities for discussion and celebration, creating wider target-language and cultural experiences for your class. There are, of course, many more events that could have been included here – the internet is an invaluable resource for finding out more about these. Use the section 'French, German and Spanish around the world' to find out which other countries speak the target language you have chosen and find out about special events and festivals held there. The 'Useful links' section introduces you to some websites I have used and found particularly helpful, or spotted while surfing the internet – I'm sure you will quickly add many more of your own.

Finally, the index table is intended as a quick-reference guide to each game/activity, giving at-a-glance key information about each one. This is intended only as a guide and to help assist in quickly identifying a suitable activity. For 'younger children' read (roughly) pre-school/Key Stage 1 and for 'older children' Key Stage 2 – however, do be aware that the suitability of an activity can depend at least as much on other factors (language-learning history, aptitude, size of group, etc.) as age so please don't treat the age categories as too prescriptive. '"Quiet" activity' refers to an activity that may help the children to settle down after a more active game or such, and I have also identified activities that involve running around etc., where you may wish to use a larger space such as the school hall, or go outside if possible.

Acknowledgements

I would like to thank Jim Siddle for his help with German, and all the 'Language in Action' children, schools and their staff who made it possible for me to try out these games.

Publisher's acknowledgements

Crown copyright material is reproduced with the permission of the Controller of HMSO and the Queen's Printer for Scotland.

Part 1
Learning objectives

Key Stage 2 Framework for Languages: Year 3 Learning objectives

Oracy		Literacy		Intercultural understanding	
Objectives	Opportunities	Objectives	Opportunities	Objectives	Opportunities
O3.1 Listen and respond to simple rhymes, stories and songs	• Identify rhyming words • Perform finger rhymes and sing songs • Join in with storytelling	L3.1 Recognise some familiar words in written form	• Understand words displayed in the classroom • Identify and read simple words • Read and understand simple messages	IU3.1 Learn about the different languages spoken by children in the school	• Increase awareness of linguistic and cultural diversity
O3.2 Recognise and respond to sound patterns and words	• Listen with care • Identify phonemes which are the same as or different from English and other known languages • Speak clearly and confidently	L3.2 Make links between some phonemes, rhymes and spellings, and read aloud familiar words	• Pronounce accurately the most commonly used characters, letters and letter strings • Read aloud a familiar sentence, rhyme or poem	IU3.2 Locate country/countries where the language is spoken	• Identify some of the countries where the language is spoken, drawing on the knowledge of class members as appropriate • Know some facts about one country, e.g. climate, main towns, famous landmarks, produce

O3.3 Perform simple communicative tasks using single words, phrases and short sentences

- Recall, retain and use vocabulary
- Ask and answer questions

L3.3 Experiment with the writing of simple words

- Write simple, familiar words using a model
- Write some single words from memory

IU3.3 Identify social conventions at home and in other cultures

- Learn about polite forms of address
- Know how to greet native speakers
- Recognise some typical names

O3.4 Listen attentively and understand instructions, everyday classroom language and praise words

- Repeat words and phrases modelled by the teacher
- Remember a sequence of spoken words
- Use physical response, mime and gesture to convey meaning and show understanding

IU3.4 Make indirect or direct contact with the country/countries where the language is spoken

- Have contact with a native speaker, including peers where appropriate
- View a video or media resource about the country
- Send an email, letter or postcard to a partner school

Key Stage 2 Framework for Languages: Year 4 Learning objectives

Oracy		Literacy		Intercultural understanding	
Objectives	Opportunities	Objectives	Opportunities	Objectives	Opportunities
O4.1 Memorise and present a short spoken text	• Learn finger rhymes, poems or a non-fiction text • Learn and say several sentences on a topic	L4.1 Read and understand a range of familiar written phrases	• Match phrases and short sentences to pictures or themes • Identify non-fiction texts by their style and layout, e.g. a recipe, a weather forecast, instructions for making or doing something, a letter, an advertisement	IU4.1 Learn about festivals and celebrations in different cultures	• Learn how children of different cultures celebrate special days • Identify similarities and differences • Learn simple phrases to celebrate festivals, drawing on the experience of fellow pupils where possible
O4.2 Listen for specific words and phrases	• Listen with care • Use physical response to show recognition and understanding of specific words and phrases	L4.2 Follow a short familiar text, listening and reading at the same time	• Make links between the spoken and written words • Identify common spelling patterns in letter strings	IU4.2 Know about some aspects of everyday life and compare them with their own	• Compare pastimes of children of different cultures and countries • Exchange information with a partner school, e.g. sports, hobbies

O4.3 Listen for sounds, rhyme and rhythm	L4.3 Read some familiar words and phrases aloud and pronounce them accurately	IU4.3 Compare traditional stories
• Identify specific sounds, e.g. rhymes, letters, phonemes, words • Compare different sounds	• Read aloud words which they use on a regular basis, e.g. numbers, days, weather • Pronounce letter strings, words and phrases accurately with good pronunciation	• Compare characteristics of simple stories between cultures • Look at the writing system of the language

O4.4 Ask and answer questions on several topics	L4.4 Write simple words and phrases using a model and some words from memory	IU4.4 Learn about ways of travelling to the country/countries
• Practise asking and answering questions with a partner • Develop and perform simple role-plays	• Write labels for work on wall display and in their books • Complete a semi-completed email message to someone in a partner school	• Revise the location of country/countries where the language is spoken • Identify a route from own locality to specified destination, drawing on the direct experience of pupils where available

Key Stage 2 Framework for Languages: Year 5 Learning objectives

Oracy		Literacy		Intercultural understanding	
Objectives	Opportunities	Objectives	Opportunities	Objectives	Opportunities
O5.1 Prepare and practise a simple conversation re-using familiar vocabulary and structures in new contexts	• Focus on correct pronunciation and intonation • Ask and answer questions • Use tone of voice and gesture to help convey meaning	L5.1 Re-read frequently a variety of short texts	• Read fiction and non-fiction texts, e.g. extracts from stories, email messages and texts from the internet	IU5.1 Compare symbols, objects or products which represent their own culture with those of another country	• Learn about symbols representing their own country, culture and community • Learn about symbols and products from another country and culture
O5.2 Understand and express simple opinion	• Agree and disagree with statements • Understand and express likes and dislikes	L5.2 Make simple sentences and short texts	• Understand that the order of words in a sentence influences the meaning • Make a sentence using single word cards • Make a short text using word and phrase cards; links to relevant NLS sentence level objectives	IU5.2 Look at further aspects of their everyday lives from the perspective of someone from another country	• Consider aspects of everyday life of children in their own and different countries • Reflect on cultural issues using empathy and imagination to understand other people's experiences

O5.3 Listen attentively and understand more complex phrases and sentences	O5.4 Prepare a short presentation on a familiar topic	L5.3 Write words, phrases and short sentences, using a reference source	IU5.3 Recognise similarities and differences between places
• Understand the main points from speech which includes unfamiliar language	• Plan and prepare – analyse what needs to be done to carry out a task • Answer in their heads questions asked to other people	• Choose words, phrases and sentences and write them into a gapped text or as picture captions • Use a bilingual dictionary to check the spelling of familiar words	• Identify geographical features of a contrasting locality • Learn about buildings and places in different countries

Key Stage 2 Framework for Languages : Year 6 Learning objectives

Oracy		Literacy		Intercultural understanding	
Objectives	Opportunities	Objectives	Opportunities	Objectives	Opportunities
O6.1 Understand the main points and simple opinions in a spoken story, song or passage	• Listen attentively, re-tell and discuss the main ideas • Agree or disagree with statements made about a spoken passage	L6.1 Read and understand the main points and some detail from a short written passage	• Read and respond to, e.g. extract from a story, an email message or song • Give true or false responses to statements about a written passage • Read descriptions of people in the school or class and identify who they are	IU6.1 Compare attitudes towards aspects of everyday life	• Recognise similarities and differences in attitudes among children in different cultures • Learn about role models for children in different cultures
O6.2 Perform to an audience	• Present a short piece of narrative either from memory or by reading aloud from text • Develop a sketch, role-play or presentation and perform to the class or an assembly	L6.2 Identify different text types and read short, authentic texts for enjoyment or information	• Read for enjoyment an email message, short story or simple text from the internet • Read and understand the gist of a familiar news story or simple magazine article	IU6.2 Recognise and understand some of the differences between people	• Discuss similarities and differences between the cultures they have learned about • Recognise and challenge stereotypes

O6.3 Understand longer and more complex phrases or sentences	L6.3 Match sound to sentences and paragraphs	IU6.3 Present information about an aspect of culture
• Re-tell using familiar language a sequence of events from a spoken passage, containing complex sentences • Understand and express reasons • Understand the gist of spoken passages containing complex sentences e.g. descriptions, information, instructions	• Use punctuation to make a sentence make sense • Listen carefully to a model, e.g. a video recording, recorded story or song, and re-constitute a sentence or paragraph using text cards • Apply most words correctly	• Perform songs, plays, dances • Use ICT to present information having a greater sense of audience

O6.4 Use spoken language confidently to initiate and sustain conversations and to tell stories	L6.4 Write sentences on a range of topics using a model	
• Participate in simple conversations on familiar topics • Describe incidents or tell stories from their own experience, in an audible voice	• Construct a short text, e.g. create a PowerPoint presentation to tell a story or give a description	

Source: www.standards.dfes.gov.uk/primary/publications/languages/framework/learning_objectives

Part 2
Games and activities

Practising
numbers and counting

Around ball

This is a fun way to teach numbers to young children and for them to practise their pronunciation.

Learning objectives

O3.2, O3.3

O4.2, O4.3

Aim

To learn numbers and practise saying them.

Vocabulary

Numbers

Resources

* Tennis ball

What to do

* Stand in a circle, with you holding a ball.
* Explain to the children they must pass the ball around the circle, repeating the numbers to one another
* Pass the ball to the child on your right saying 'one' in the target language (TL); they repeat this, passing it to the person on their right, and so on round the circle until it gets back to you.
* For the next round, say 'two' as you pass the ball and this is repeated around the circle...
* See how quickly you can move the ball around the circle, without dropping it – if the ball is dropped, it goes back to the start and you begin again with 'one'

Variation

For children who already know their numbers, divide the group into two team circles which compete to see who can complete 5, 10, 20 ... rounds the quickest.

Ball·toss counting

Another ball game for practising counting.

Learning objectives

O3.2, O3.3

O4.2

Aim

To play a throw-and-catch game while practising counting.

Vocabulary

Numbers

Resources

• Tennis ball

What to do

• Standing in a circle, the first child throws the ball to any other child in the circle, saying 'one' in TL.
• The child who catches the ball must toss the ball into the air once, counting 'one' before they in turn throw the ball to a second child, saying 'two'.
• The child who has the ball now must toss it into the air twice, counting 'one, two' as they do so.
• Continue to practise all the numbers known so far.

Cross-curriculum link

PE

Bean hunt

A counting game with a party feel.

Learning objectives

O3.3

Aim

To find beans etc. hidden around the room and to count them.

Vocabulary

Numbers

Resources

- Dried beans/pennies/similar small objects
- Paper cups

What to do

- Before the children enter the classroom, hide dried beans in nooks and crannies around the room (behind doors, under furniture/ cushions, between books, on windowsills – anywhere that is safe to search).
- Children enter and each is given a paper cup to collect beans and sent on a search-and-recover mission.
- Give children 5 or 10 minutes to find as many beans as possible.
- When time is up, each child counts their beans in TL – the one with the most wins.

Beanbags

An art-and-craft activity, the results of which can be used many times.

Learning objectives

O3.3

L4.3

Aim

To make beanbags and use them in a number of games.

Vocabulary

Numbers, colours ...

Resources

- Socks
- Rice/dried beans/lentils
- Small freezer bags
- String

What to do

- Give each child an old sock, some rice/dried beans, lentils, etc., a small freezer bag and some string.
- Fill the freezer bag with rice/beans, tie securely and roll up in the sock, which should also be tied.
- To play, children stand in a line and throw their beanbags on to sheets of paper/card which have numbers or pictures on them – the children must say out loud the TL word for the number/picture their beanbag lands on.

Variation

For older children with a good knowledge of numbers, place paper plates – on which you have written large numbers or simple maths equations – face down on the floor. Children take turns to throw their beanbag on to a plate, turn it over and say the number/solve the equation in TL.

Cross-curriculum links

Art, maths

Bingo

An old favourite which children of all ages love, and which is a useful 'staple' for practising all kinds of vocabulary.

Learning objectives

03.2

04.2

Aim

To listen out for the numbers or pictures on your bingo card.

Vocabulary

Numbers, colours, animals ...

Resources

- Bingo cards or paper
- Counters or pens for crossing off

What to do

- Hand out pre-printed bingo cards to each child.
- Alternatively, give each child a photocopied blank grid two squares by eight (or ask them to draw one) and ask them to fill in numbers themselves (specify that they must be between 1 and ... 20, 50, 100).
- Make sure each child has either a pen/pencil or access to counters.
- As you call out numbers in TL, children must cross them off their card (or, if you wish to re-use the cards, place counters over the numbers).

Variations

- You can use bingo to practise more or less any vocabulary area – e.g. ask the children to draw the animals or foods you have learnt.
- Ask a child to take the place of the teacher and call out the numbers/words.

Cross-curriculum link

To turn this into a fun role-play for a drama lesson, children can dress up and pretend to be real people down at the local bingo hall!

Body-part count

A party-style game for practising small numbers.

Learning objectives

03.2, 03.4

04.2

Aim

To listen for numbers and respond accordingly.

Vocabulary

Numbers

Resources

- CD player and music

What to do

- Children walk or dance around the room as music plays.
- When the music stops, call out a number between 'one' and 'ten' in TL – the children have to position themselves so that this number of parts of their body are in contact with the floor.
- Encourage children to be as original as possible with their choices, e.g. for 'two' – instead of simply standing on two feet, try one knee and one elbow; one foot and one hand, etc.

Cross-curriculum link

PE

Call ball

Yet another counting ball game!

Learning objectives

O3.2, O3.3, IU3.3

Aim

To recognise and respond to numbers.

Vocabulary

Numbers

Resources

- Tennis ball

What to do

- Give each child a number and tell them to spread out around the room.
- One player begins by bouncing the ball high into the air and calling out another player's number in TL.
- As soon as the ball leaves the bouncer's hand, the other players run away except the one whose number has been called, who must try to catch the ball before it hits the ground again.
- If successful, this child then bounces the ball calling out another number, whose owner must rush back to try to catch the ball before it hits the ground ...
- If a child misses their number, they must leave the game.

Variation

Allocate each child a name from a TL country and call these out instead of numbers.

Card hunt

A number game which also allows children to practise some game-playing vocabulary.

Learning objectives

O3.3

O4.4

Aim

To engage in a simple question and answer game.

Vocabulary

Numbers, colours, game playing

Resources

- Two packs of playing cards

What to do

- Before the children enter the classroom, hide all 52 cards from one deck around the room. Separate one further deck into red and black cards.
- Once the children have entered, divide them into two equal teams. Give each member of 'red' team a red card and each member of 'black' team a black one.
- Each player must search the room for the card which exactly corresponds to the one in their hand. Any other cards discovered along the way should be left in place. When a child finds the matching card, they bring it to you and must answer questions in TL like 'What colour is it?', 'What number is it?' and 'What suit does it belong to?'
- If answered successfully, the child is then given another card from their team colour pile.
- The winning team is the one that finds all the cards in their colour first.

Concentration

As the name suggests, this game requires real focus and can keep children quiet for quite some time!

Learning objectives

O3.2, O3.3

O4.2

Aim

To practise saying numbers while keeping to a rhythm.

Vocabulary

Numbers

What to do

- Ask children to sit in a circle and then give each child a consecutive number, working your way round the circle.
- Begin a rhythm in 4/4 time, where the first beat is created by slapping thighs, second by clapping hands, and third and fourth by snapping fingers on the left then right hand.
- Once the group can sustain this rhythm together, pick someone to go first.
- On the first snap (beat 3) this child says their own number in TL (say 'four'), on the second snap they say another's (say 'seven'). Child 7 then says 'seven' on their first snap and another's number on the second snap ...
- Any child who speaks at the wrong time, breaks the rhythm, says a wrong number, etc. is out. That number is then removed from the game and can't be used!

Cross-curriculum link

Music

Copy counting

Children sometimes need an additional focus when learning or practising counting!

Learning objectives

03.2, 03.3

Aim

To practise saying numbers.

Vocabulary

Numbers

What to do

- Stand in a circle.
- I show the child on my left an action while saying 'one' in TL. They must then turn to their left, repeat or mirror the action and say 'two'. That child repeats the action to their left saying 'three' ...

Variation

Numbers need to be practised often. Have a few moments in each lesson where you count: children in the group, coins for shopping, steps to reach the other side of the room, black shoes, children with fair hair ...

Counting blocks

Children love the atmosphere of tension created by this game.

Learning objectives

03.2, 03.3

Aim

To practise counting.

Vocabulary

Numbers

Resources

* A game of Jenga, or similar

What to do

* Ask the children to sit in a circle and place the Jenga© tower on the floor in the centre.
* Taking turns, each child removes a block from the tower, counting aloud in TL with each turn.
* The object of the game is to prevent the tower from toppling over, by removing the blocks as carefully as possible.
* When the tower does fall (inevitably!) whoever's turn it was that caused it to topple must answer a TL question.
* Rebuild the tower and begin a new round!

Variation

You can also play this game in reverse, each child placing a block (and counting aloud), so gradually building the tower from scratch until it falls over.

Dice games

Use dice to create original and exciting ways of practising pronunciation of numbers, counting and basic maths. You should impose a rule that all speaking and counting (aloud) during these games must be done in TL.

Learning objectives

O3.2, O3.3, O3.4, L3.1, L3.2

Vocabulary

Numbers, game-playing, clothing

Resources

- Dice (a maximum of six is needed for each group of players; the number of dice needed for each game is shown in brackets)
- Paper and pens
- Items of clothing (for 'Get dressed dice')

What to do

Die rolling (one or two dice)

- Children call out in TL which number from 1–6 they think the die will land on.
- Double dice: children roll two dice and call out numbers from 2–12.
- If a child guesses correctly, they get a point and another go – if not, pass on to the next player.

Fifty (two dice)

- Players roll two dice. You only score if doubles are thrown.
- Double 1, 2, 4 or 5 scores 5 points.
- Double 6 scores 25 points.

- Double 3 wipes out the player's entire previous score and the player must start again from 0.
- The first player to reach 50 is the winner.

Chicago (two dice)

- The object is to roll the 11 possible totals using two dice, in sequence (ie. 2, 3, 4, 5, 6, 7, 8, 9, 10, 11 and finally 12).
- The first player throws both dice with the aim of getting 2 (two 1s). If successful, a point is awarded.
- Each player has a chance to roll 2, then in the next round they must try for 3, then 4 ...
- Each time players are successful, they are awarded a point.
- Any combination adding up to the desired total is fine (e.g. to score 7: 1 and 6, 2 and 5, 3 and 4 are all acceptable).
- The first player to reach 12 wins – or, if you are playing against the clock, players add up their score when time is up and the highest scorer wins.

Round the clock (two dice)

- The object is to roll the numbers 1 to 12 in sequence.
- Each player rolls one die to establish who goes first (the highest number rolled).
- Each player rolls two dice (once only) per turn.
- The first player rolls both dice, hoping to get a 1 on either die. If not, they have to try again on the following round. If successful, on their next go they try to get a 2 – which they can achieve either on one die or as a combination of both. If successful, they try for 3 on the next round, etc. ...
- If a player gets two of the numbers needed in a single go, they both count – e.g. if the player has already rolled a 1 and then on their next go they roll 2 and 3.
- Players continue taking turns until someone reaches 12 – they are the winner.

Going to Boston (three dice)

- Players all roll a die to establish who goes first (highest starts).
- First player rolls three dice and sets aside the die with the highest number. (If two, or even three, dice show the highest number, still only one is set aside.)
- The same player then rolls the two remaining dice and again sets aside the highest.
- Then the same player throws the last die, and the total of the three dice is the player's score for that round.
- When each player has completed a three-roll turn, the game is over. The highest score wins.
- Or, if playing against the clock, you can keep going until time is up.
- Alternatively, play until an agreed total score is reached by the winner.

Get dressed dice (one die and a collection of dressing-up clothes)

- This game is like 'Round the clock' but only using one die.
- Clothing is laid out in the centre of a circle, several each of six different items (e.g. pairs of gloves, scarves, hats, sunglasses, belts).
- Allocate each item of clothing a number, e.g.: 1 = right glove, 2 = hat, 3 = scarf, 4 = left glove, 5 = sunglasses, 6 = belt.
- Each child rolls the die, trying to get 1. If successful, they put on the first item (right glove).
- If they do not roll a 1, play passes to the next child, who also tries to roll a 1.
- Once a child has succeeded in getting a 1 and put on their right glove, on their next turn they try to roll a 2 ... and so on.
- The first child to get fully dressed in all six items wins.

Spelling dice (six dice)

- Choose a six- (or less) letter TL word – with no repeated letters.
- Each number on the die corresponds to a letter in the word, e.g. for *chaise* 1 = c, 2 = h, 3 = a ... Write these up on the board.
- The first player rolls all six dice. If any of the dice shows 1 (corresponding to the first letter of the word) the player scores 5 points. If there's a 2 as well, corresponding to the second letter, the player scores another 5.

- As long as the numbers follow in sequence, the player gets an additional 5 points for each 'letter' in the word.
- A 5-point bonus is given for spelling the whole word in one go.
- If more than one die shows the same number, only one of them counts towards the score. So if a player rolls 1, 2, 2, 3, 5, 5 the score is 15 points for 1, 2, 3 (c, h, a)
- A roll of three 1s (c's) wipes out player's entire score so far.
- Each player gets one roll per turn.
- Letters scored on previous turns don't carry over, so each child must start each new turn with a 1.
- The winner is the highest scorer after a certain number of rounds, or the first to reach an agreed score (e.g. 100).

Drop dead (five dice)

- The first player rolls five dice.
- If a 2 or 5 show up, the die or dice showing the offending number(s) is/are removed.
- If neither a 2 nor a 5 appear, the player adds together the numbers showing on all five of the dice.
- The same player then rolls the remaining dice, adding points to their score or eliminating dice, until all the dice are 'dead'.
- This player then 'drops dead' and it's the next player's turn.
- The player with the most points after everyone has dropped dead wins.

Pig (one die)

- The aim is to roll a total score of 100.
- The first player rolls the die as many times as they like, adding together the numbers shown to give their score, until they decide to end their go and pass on to the next player.
- If any player rolls a 1, their entire score for that turn is wiped out, their turn ends, and play passes to the next player.
- Each player must decide for himself when to stop. A player could have their score wiped out on the first roll by getting a 1, or they could reach the winning score (100) in their first go by *not* rolling a 1.
- If a player stops before reaching 100 (and before being knocked out) the next player knows there's no point stopping until at least reaching that same score.

- If the second player manages to do that, then the next player knows how many they have got to beat ... and so on
- Play continues until someone reaches 100, or (if playing against the clock) until all players have had a chance to roll, in which case the highest scorer wins.

Cross-curriculum link

Maths

Dominoes

Children can make their own set of dominoes from stiff card.

Learning objectives

O3.2, O3.3, L3.1, L3.2, L3.3

Aim

To practise saying or reading numbers or other vocabulary.

Vocabulary

Numbers, any

Resources

* Game of dominoes

What to do

* Play the game as per the normal rules. (If unsure of these see www.domino-games.com)
* Children must say the TL number aloud as they place each domino down.

Variations

* As a craft activity, allow children to make their own set of dominoes.
* Try writing the numbers in words and matching them to the correct digit.
* Dominoes do not necessarily have to be used to match numbers: you can draw a picture/shape/colour on one half of the domino and a word on the other (see Enchanted Learning website, www.enchantedlearning.com, for a printable set of colour dominoes to make in French or Spanish).

Cross-curriculum links

Art, maths

Embouteillage

A fast-paced game requiring maximum concentration.

Learning objectives

O3.2, O3.3, L3.2

O4.3, L4.3

Aim

To practise words that are difficult to pronounce, while counting.

Vocabulary

Numbers; words that children find particularly difficult to pronounce

What to do

- Sitting in a circle, children begin to count in TL round to the right, saying a number each.
- Whenever a multiple of 7, or a number with 7 in it, is reached it must be replaced with a word the child finds difficult to say (e.g. *embouteillage*). So 7, 14, 17, 21, 27, 28 ... (any number in the 70s must also be replaced).
- Any number that is both a multiple of 7 and has 7 in it (70, 77) must be replaced by two words.
- Go as fast as possible – if someone replaces a wrong number, or misses one, they are out of the game.

Variation

Saying the difficult-to-pronounce word on multiples of 5 / numbers with 5 in is slightly easier.

Cross-curriculum link

Maths

Get into groups of...

This game helps beginners to quickly recognise numbers out of sequence. It is great fun as it has a party-game feel to it.

Learning objectives

03.2, 03.4

Aim

To recognise and respond to numbers out of sequence.

Vocabulary

Numbers

Resources

● CD player and music

What to do

● Start with the children walking or dancing around the room with music playing.
● When you stop the music, call out a number in TL and the children have to organise themselves as quickly as possible into groups of that number.
● Any children left over are out; start the music again.
● Keep going until you are down to one last group or, if you don't mind a competitive aspect, until there is only one child left who is the winner.
● Note: this game really brings out the bossy-boots in some children, so insist that all instructions and counting be done in TL!

Cross-curriculum link

PE

Guess how many

A guessing game to practise small numbers.

Learning objectives

03.2, 03.3

Aim

To practise saying and recognising small numbers.

Vocabulary

Numbers

Resources

- Small objects that can be held behind the back in one hand – pens, beans, coins ...

What to do

- A child stands at the front of the class where there is a pile of pens/beans/coins.
- With their back to the class, the child takes a few objects, counting how many have been taken, and turns to face the class hiding the objects behind their back
- The rest of the group put up their hands to guess how many objects there are (in TL) – the first child to guess correctly is the next one up.

Variation

The children can perform basic maths operations using the pens/beans etc. – if the group knows that the child standing at the front had ten coins behind their back and then takes four away, how many will there be now?

Cross-curriculum link

Maths

Hand-clap circle

A counting game that requires concentration.

Learning objectives

03.2, 03.3
04.2

Aim

To practise counting.

Vocabulary

Numbers

What to do

- Standing in a circle, ask the children to hold their left hand with palm facing up and their right with palm facing down.
- Each child places the palm of their left hand under the right palm of person to their left.
- With their right hand, the first child claps the left palm of the person to their right saying 'one' in TL, who passes it on to the next person saying 'two' ...
- The numbers/claps are passed round as quickly as possible, until a child says an agreed TL 'code' word, at which point the direction of play changes and counting starts again from 'one'.

Hopscotch

Another well-known playground game that lends itself to TL number practice.

Learning objectives

03.2, 03.3

Aim

To practise counting in sequence and with numbers missing.

Vocabulary

Numbers

Resources

- Chalk
- Beanbag

What to do

- Draw a hopscotch grid (see diagram) on the playground with chalk or on the earth using a stick.
- The first player tries to throw the beanbag into square 1. If they fail, the next player has a go.
- If they manage to land the beanbag in square 1, they hop to the end of the grid and back, missing out the square with the beanbag in, calling out each number in TL as they hop on to it.
- When they reach the square with the beanbag in, they pick it up and carry on to the end.
- If they can do this without making a mistake, then they can try and throw their marker into square 2 and carry on in the same way. When the player makes a mistake, it is the next person's turn.
- The first person to complete the grid is the winner.

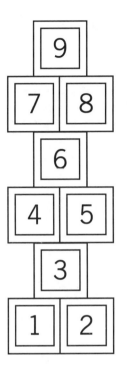

Cross-curriculum link

PE

Japanese hopscotch

Fun, if you have enough space.

Learning objectives

O3.2, O3.3

Aim

To practise counting.

Vocabulary

Numbers

Resources

- Chalk or sheets of paper numbered 1–19

What to do

- Draw a 19-square grid on the ground using chalk, or if playing indoors lay out 19 sheets of plain paper each with a number written on.
- Children line up in front of square 1.
- The first player hops through all 19 squares, calling out the numbers in TL and must land in the middle of each square, not on the lines.
- Player 1 stops to write their initials in any square. When they reach the end they walk back to the end of the line.
- Player 2 hops along the grid, but cannot land on the square bearing player 1's initials but instead must hop over it. Player 2 also initials a square of their own and returns to the line.
- The game continues with any player who makes it through to the end of the grid initialling the square of their choice, until it becomes impossible to hop through the grid.
- The player who 'owns' the most squares at the end wins.

Keepy·uppy

A counting game that can be boisterous!

Learning objectives

O3.2, O3.3

Aim

To practise counting while keeping a ball/balloon from touching the ground.

Vocabulary

Numbers

Resources

- Large sponge ball or balloon

What to do

- Children stand in a circle and each child is given a number
- Child 1 steps into the middle of the circle and bats the ball into the air, calling out 'one' in TL.
- Child 2 has the time it takes for the ball to bounce *once* to step into the circle and bat it up again, saying 'two' ... and so on.
- If anyone fails to reach the ball and call out their number in time, start again with 'one'.
- Continue until everyone has taken a turn.

Variations

- For older children (if you have enough space) try not to let the ball touch the ground *at all*. The children spread out all around the room and anyone can bat the ball up into the air, so everyone must be alert the whole time – don't forget to shout out numbers as you go!
- For younger children (or if space is restricted) a balloon is best because it takes longer to float down to the ground. Also they tend to get rather excited and a balloon generally does less damage!
- If the children know higher numbers, continue the game until someone drops the ball/misses their turn. Every few lessons try again to beat the class record!

Cross-curriculum link

PE

Ladders

A listening game for practising comprehension of numbers.

Learning objectives

O3.2, O3.3

O4.2

Aim

To listen, respond to and understand numbers.

Vocabulary

Numbers

Resources

- CD player and music

What to do

- Divide the class into two teams and ask them to sit on the ground in two lines facing each other, with legs extended and feet touching.
- Give each pair of children (one from each team) a TL number.
- Call out a number at random.
- Upon hearing it, the pair who have been given that number must stand up, run down the middle of the two teams along the 'ladder' of legs, split at the bottom, run along the outside of their team line, and back down to their original place.
- The first child back in position must answer a simple TL question in order to win their team a point.

Variation

Should you have a child left over, give them the job of calling out numbers and/or asking the questions.

Cross-curriculum link

PE

Multiple counting

This counting game also tests children on their knowledge of multiples, so they have to concentrate extra hard!

Learning objectives

O3.2, O3.4

O4.2

Aims

- To practise counting and recognise numbers.
- To understand and recognise multiples.
- To make an appropriate physical response to a command.

Vocabulary

Numbers

What to do

- Children sit in a circle.
- Begin by counting around the circle in TL, each child saying their own number out loud.
- Explain to children that their number will remain the same for the duration of the game.
- Count around the circle again, but this time around, any child whose number is a multiple of 3 must clap as they say their number.
- Next time around, keep the claps in but add a foot stamp for multiples of 4, then a head nod for multiples of 5 ...

Variation

The more advanced the children's knowledge of maths, the more multiples you can add!

Cross-curriculum link

Maths

Number fishing

A firm favourite – children of all ages love this game.

Learning objectives

03.2, 03.3

Aim

To recognise and practise numbers.

Vocabulary

Numbers

Resources

- Set of 20 fish cut from coloured card, numbered 1–20, with paperclip 'tails'
- Two fishing rods (made from 1 m. (3 ft) lengths of garden bamboo, string and two small magnets)

What to do

- Place the fish face down and have the children sit in two teams around the 'fishpond'.
- Give the first child from each team a fishing rod.
- The first child from team 1 stands over the pond with the rod and must catch a fish using the magnet, lifting it out of the pond and reading the number out in TL.
- If correct, this child keeps hold of the fish and the first child from team 2 takes a turn.
- If incorrect, the fish is returned to the pond and the opposite team take their turn.
- When the pond is empty the team with the most fish has won.

Variation

To turn this into a non-competitive activity simply pass the rod around the circle, each child taking a turn to catch a fish and read out its number, until the pond is empty.

Number race

A counting warm-up.

Learning objectives

O3.2, O3.3
O4.2

Aim

To listen to and recognise numbers.

Vocabulary

Numbers

What to do

- Children stand in a circle.
- Go round the circle tapping each child on the head and numbering them (in TL).
- When you call out their number, the child has to run clockwise around the circle and back to their original position.
- The child must then sit down cross-legged.
- Continue until you have only one child left standing.

Cross-curriculum link

PE

Odd bean

A gap-filler for practising counting.

Learning objectives

03.2, 03.3

Aim

To practise counting.

Vocabulary

Numbers, game-playing

Resources

- Some bags with dried beans in (or similar)

What to do

- Children sit in pairs.
- Each child has a bag with 20 dried beans in.
- Player A reaches into the bag, takes a handful of beans, hides them in their fist, and asks in TL 'Odd or even?'
- Player B takes a guess.
- If correct, B wins the beans and it's their go. If wrong, B must hand over to player A the same number of beans as would have been won.
- The child at the end with the most beans is the winner.

Cross-curriculum link

Maths

One, two, three

This is a quick warm-up number activity which promotes listening in young children.

Learning objectives

O3.2, O3.4

O4.2

Aim

To respond to numbers being spoken.

Vocabulary

Numbers

What to do

- Sitting in a circle, each child is given a TL number – 'one', 'two' or 'three' (ensure an equal-ish quantity of each).
- Call out either 'one', 'two' or 'three' in TL.
- All the children with that number must get up and run clockwise around the circle, ending up back in their original place.
- The last one back to their place is out and leaves the circle.

Variations

This game can also be used to practise different vocabulary areas. For example, the children could be given the names of foods, French-speaking countries or new verbs.

Cross-curriculum link

PE

Psychic counting

A quiet activity that can really focus the minds of the group

Learning objectives

O3.2, O3.3

O4.2

Aim

To practise counting

Vocabulary

Numbers

What to do

- Seated in a circle, everyone closes their eyes.
- For a few moments just observe a calming silence
- One by one children begin to call out TL numbers in sequence, trying to 'sense' when there is a gap for them to speak
- If more than one person speaks the same number at the same time, start again from 'one'.

Practising specific vocabulary areas

Action verbs

This drama activity enables children to practise action verbs in a fun and original way.

Learning objectives

O3.2, O3.3, L3.1

O4.2, L4.3

Aim

To listen to and understand action verbs and respond accordingly.

Vocabulary

Action verbs

What to do

- Teach the children a list of approximately eight action verbs in TL – examples might include '*eat*', '*work*', '*dance*', '*clean*' … If you want to introduce them in written form, write them up on the board.
- Seat the children like a theatre audience with a small 'stage' area.
- A child takes the stage and mentally chooses one of the verbs from the list.
- One by one, audience members feed them adverbs in English (you may need to explain or recap with the group what an adverb is) – the actor must then act out the verb in the manner directed. For example, if the verb is *manger*, the class can instruct the actor to do it 'noisily', 'shyly', 'stupidly'… until someone guesses the verb.
- Whoever guesses correctly takes the next turn on the stage.

Cross-curriculum links

Drama, literacy

Let's march

A nice warm-up for a cold day!

Learning objectives

O3.2, O3.3
O4.2, O4.3

Aim

To listen, respond to and understand action verbs.

Vocabulary

Action verbs

What to do

- Ask the children to spread out around the room.
- Demonstrate a variety of action verbs – marching, jumping, running, spinning, bending, waving, wiggling ... – and teach the TL name of each one.
- As the children move around the room, call out instructions (e.g. *marcher*, *sauter*) which the children must repeat back to you in time with their own movements.
- As the children become familiar with the words, alternate fast-talk with slow-talk instructions.
- Pick a child to be the leader themselves, giving the TL verbs as instructions.

Cross-curriculum link

PE

Warm-up verbs

An energetic warm-up for young children.

Learning objectives

O3.2, O3.4

Aim

To respond to different action verbs in TL.

Vocabulary

Action verbs

What to do

- Children spread out around the room.
- Begin by asking the children to walk around the room and say the verb 'walk' in TL – ask the children to repeat the word in rhythm as they walk around.
- Feed the class different action verbs in TL, e.g.: walk, run, skip, hop, jump ... demonstrating each one – the children repeat each one as they do the actions.
- Once they have practised each verb a couple of times, stop demonstrating, and give the instructions more and more quickly.

Cross-curriculum link

PE

Animal drawing

Young children love drawing – they will be proud to take their pictures home, and children who are old enough should label their drawing in TL.

Learning objectives

O3.2, O3.3, L3.3

O4.2

Aim

To practise the names of animals.

Vocabulary

Animals

Resources

- Blackboard and chalk, whiteboard, or paper and pens

What to do

- One at a time children come up to the board/take a piece of blank paper and a pen and begin to draw an animal – the rest of the class must raise their hands to guess in TL which animal is being drawn.
- Whoever guesses correctly takes the next turn.

Variation

If your class is very big and it would take too long for everyone to have a turn, simply give each child a piece of paper and a pen and say the animal names in TL one by one for them to draw.

Cross-curriculum link

Art

Animal matching

This animal jigsaw game also encourages children to count out loud.

Learning objectives

O3.3, O3.4

O4.2

Aim

- To practise saying numbers out loud.
- To practise the names of six animals.

Vocabulary

Animals, numbers, game-playing

Resources

- Six animal jigsaws, each with six pieces
- Dice

What to do

- Number the pieces of each jigsaw one to six (using stickers or simply write them on the back in pencil).
- Teach the names of the animals in TL.
- Lay out the pieces face up. Children take it in turns to shake a die, saying out loud in TL the number they have rolled.
- Whoever rolls 1 can select the corresponding piece no.1 of an animal of their choice; they then have to wait until they roll 2 to add the next piece etc.
- The first one to complete an animal, and say its name correctly, wins.

Animal mime

Young children love to act like different animals; older children can be more challenged in this drama activity.

Learning objectives

O3.3

O4.2

Aim

To practise the names of a variety of animals.

Vocabulary

Animals

What to do

- One by one, children stand before the rest of the group and act out an animal; the rest of the group have to guess which one (in TL).
- For older children: without making give-away sounds, they have to emulate the 'essence' of the animal, capturing its movement and energy.

Cross-curriculum link

Drama

Animal picture hop

Needs a nice clear space!

Learning objectives

03.2, 03.3
04.2

Aim

To listen and respond to the names of animals.

Vocabulary

Animals

Resources

* Set of 20 A4 animal picture cards (four each of five animals)

What to do

* Lay the animal cards out all over the floor.
* As you call out the names of the animals in TL the children must hop on to the correct picture and remain there on one leg until the next one is called out ...
* Anyone who falls over/hops on to the wrong animal is out.
* When children are out, they must call the next animal name.

Variation

- Of course you are not limited to using animal vocabulary here, you can use pictures of anything – or even numbers.

- Although it may seem extravagant to print out 20 black-and-white pictures on to coloured card (a different colour for each animal) these cards come in handy for all sorts of gap-filler games. You can use them simply for teaching the animals' names in the first place. If you laminate them they will last a lot longer, *but* don't let children play this game in socks as they may slip.

Animal sculptures

For young children.

Learning objectives

O3.2, O3.3, O3.4
O4.2

Aim

To understand and practise the names of different animals.

Vocabulary

Animals

What to do

- Ask children to get into pairs and number each pair 1 and 2.
- Explain that child 1 is a sculptor and child 2 is a lump of clay. Child 2 begins curled up on the ground
- As you call out the names of different animals in TL, the artists must 'mould' their clay into the shape of the animal – explain that the 'sculptors' must be gentle, and that the 'clay' should try to be as relaxed as possible and not try to move their body independently.
- After a few turns, children 1 and 2 reverse roles.
- Then ask each 'sculptor' individually to sculpt their 'clay' into an animal: the rest of the group must guess which animal is being depicted.

Cross-curriculum link

Drama

Disco zoo

This very silly dancing activity enables children to practise the names of animals.

Learning objectives

O3.3, O3.4

O4.2

Aim

To practise animal names.

Vocabulary

Animals

Resources

* CD player and music

What to do

* Children spread out around the room.
* Ask the children to think of an animal whose TL name they have learnt, and to keep it secret.
* Explain to the children that, while the music plays, they will each portray their particular animal as they imagine it would dance – getting on down at the local disco!
* The children must observe each other's behaviour and afterwards ask them to identify which animals each other was portraying – you could offer points for each correct guess.

Cross-curriculum links

PE, Drama

Gaelle's animal bingo

A fun way of practising animal names.

Learning objectives

03.2, 03.3

04.2

Aim

To recognise the names of animals.

Vocabulary

Animals

Resources

- An envelope for each child containing ten small pictures of animals.
- A printed bingo grid for each child with six squares.

What to do

- Distribute the bingo cards and envelopes.
- Ask the children to take six of the animal pictures from their envelope and place them on the six squares of their grid.
- Say the TL names of the animals one by one – if a child has placed that animal on their grid they must turn it face down.
- When all their animals have been turned face down the player shouts out TL equivalent of 'bingo!' – the first child to shout out wins the game.

Rabbit, duck, elephant

A gap-filler or warm-up which focuses the group.

Learning objectives

03.2, 03.3
04.2

Aim

To practise animal names.

Vocabulary

Animals

What to do

- Children stand in a circle.
- Explain that it takes three children to create an animal and how each animal is made.
- Stand in the centre of the circle and point to one child, saying either 'rabbit', 'duck' or 'elephant' in TL.
- Depending on which animal is said, the child pointed to must display a rabbit's buck teeth using two fingers pointing downwards, a duck's bill using hands, or an elephant's trunk using one arm, while the child either side must contribute a bunny ear each (arm held up stiff on top of the middle child's head), webbed feet (right and left hand splayed out from the middle child's waist) or elephant ears (one hand each splayed out on top of the middle child's head).
- The three children must complete the animal before you finish counting to three.
- Whoever does the wrong movement or does not complete the animal in time takes your place in the centre.

Racing animals

This can get hot and sweaty!

Learning objectives

O3.2, O3.3
O4.2

Aim

To understand and respond to animal names.

Vocabulary

Animals

What to do

- Children line up along one side of the room.
- Call out an animal name in TL and the children must then travel as fast as possible to the other end of the room, doing the appropriate animal action:
  - spider: link arms back-to-back, one person moving forwards, the other backwards
  - frog: leapfrog over each other
  - crab: walking on hands and feet with arched back
  - pig: one child carries another piggy-back
  - lizard: wheelbarrow-style, holding partner's ankles
  - flamingo: hopping on one leg
  - snake: slithering on stomach
  - elephant: run waving one arm around like a trunk
  - ostrich: arm up in the air like long neck.

Variation

The children can make up their own ways of travelling as an animal across the room.

Cross·curriculum link

PE

Visiting the zoo

Another animal activity for young children.

Learning objectives

03.2, 03.3

04.2

Aim

To say and recognise the names of animals.

Vocabulary

Animals

What to do

- Divide the class into small groups of two or three children but keep two children separate.
- Ask each group to stay together and position themselves around the room.
- Explain that each group represents a different zoo animal but that they won't know which animal they are until told.
- The two children kept apart at the start are a child and its parent – they are visiting the zoo.
- As they walk around the room, the parent points out the different 'animals' in their cages in TL: 'Look, the monkeys/elephants/snakes!'
- As soon as they learn which animal they are, the caged creatures begin to act out the animal, making the appropriate animal noises.

Variation

If the children are very young or in the early stages of language learning it may be easier for you to play the part of the parent and do the talking – the children can simply respond to the animal names.

Cross-curriculum link

Drama

Blindfold body drawing

This is an imaginative, student-led way for children to practise their vocabulary in a specific area.

Learning objectives

03.3, 03.4

04.2

Aims

- To practise saying the names of different parts of the body.
- To practise listening to these words and responding accordingly.

Vocabulary

Parts of the body

Resources

- Plain paper
- Pencils
- Scarf etc. for blindfold

What to do

- Children sit in a circle and one child wears a blindfold.
- The blindfolded child is given a blank sheet of paper and a pencil.
- One at a time, other children in the group call out parts of the body in TL.
- The blindfolded child must draw the correct body part, attempting to end up with a complete drawing of a person. Of course, being blindfolded the parts don't quite fit together and you end up with some very funny drawings!

Variations

- To save time this activity can also be performed in pairs, where one child wears a blindfold (or simply closes their eyes) and the other gives the names of body parts for their partner to draw. Then swap over.
- This game can be used to practise almost any vocabulary area, not just the names of body parts.
- You can, of course, omit the blindfold altogether to create a more artistic challenge for the children.

Cross-curriculum link

Art

Body drawing

A fun art activity for young children.

Learning objectives

L3.3

L4.4

Aim

To write the names of body parts in their correct places on to a drawing.

Vocabulary

Body parts

Resources

- Large roll of paper, such as wall lining paper
- Pencils and pens

What to do

- Each child lies down on a piece of paper that is wide and long enough to fit their whole body on.
- Draw around each child (this is best done by an adult, but if the children are drawing round each other, use pencil to avoid staining clothes).
- The child can then colour themselves in, including hair, facial features, clothes ...
- Help each child to label the different parts of the body in TL.

Variation

Use this activity for drawing and labelling items of clothing.

Cross-curriculum link

Art

Face touch

An interesting way to learn and practise the different parts of the face.

Learning objectives

O3.2, O3.3

Aim

To practise saying the names of facial features.

Vocabulary

Parts of the face

What to do

- Instruct children to wash their hands first!
- In pairs, children sit opposite each other – child A closes their eyes and feels gently over child B's face, saying the TL names of the facial features as they are touched.
- Switch roles.

Knots & Tangles

A listening activity.

Learning objectives

O3.2, O3.3
O4.2

Aim

To listen to and understand the names of body parts.

Vocabulary

Parts of the body

Resources

- CD player and music

What to do

- As the music plays, the children dance around the room.
- Explain to children that when you stop the music they must find a partner as quickly as possible.
- Call out a part of the body in TL, e.g. 'hand' – each pair must touch their hands together.
- When they have had a few practices, make the commands harder by giving two body parts such as 'knee to elbow', 'big toe to nose', 'head to head', 'back to back', 'tummy to little finger'.
- Children must find a new partner each time.

Variation

For an element of competition, the last pair to complete the action each time is out.

Cross-curriculum link

PE

Simon says ...

This well-known game is extremely popular due to its competitive nature; children will request it again and again!

Learning objectives

03.2, 03.3, 03.4

04.2

Aim

To practise and understand parts of the body.

Vocabulary

Parts of the body

What to do

- Children stand in a circle.
- Begin with a recap of all the body parts the group have learnt in TL.
- Explain the rules: you will be asking the children to touch various different parts of their body; however the children must *only* follow your command if it begins with the phrase 'Simon says touch ...'

French	*Jacques a dit touchez ...(le nez)*
German	*Simon sagt tippt euch an ... (die Nase)*
Spanish	*Simon dice toca ... (la nariz)*

- Give commands, e.g: 'Simon says touch your nose' then slip in one without 'Simon says', e.g. 'Touch your head'.
- Anyone who follows a command which does not begin 'Simon says touch ... ' or who touches the wrong body part is out and must sit down.
- Continue until only one child is left standing – they are the winner!

Variation

Once children have got the hang of the format and the language being used, nominate different children to give the commands – one child can lead a whole game, or alternatively make each child who goes out the next to give a command.

Clothes shop

This dressing-up activity encourages active role-play.

Learning objectives

O4.1, O4.4
O5.1
O6.2

Aim

To use clothes to practise key phrases and vocabulary.

Vocabulary

Clothes, politeness phrases, numbers …

Resources

* Selection of dressing-up clothing

What to do

* Sort clothes into 'departments' as per a clothes shop – hats, shoes, bags, etc.
* Children take it in turns to be shopkeeper/customer, asking for an item in TL and trying it on, saying if it's too small/big, asking how much … etc.

Variation

In your clothes shop encourage children to role-play paying for things in euros.

Cross-curriculum link

Maths

Suitcase game

Another variation on 'My grandmother went to market'.

Learning objectives

O3.2, O3.3

Aim

To practise and remember a list of TL words.

Vocabulary

Clothes

Resources

- Selection of items of clothing
- Suitcase (or large cardboard box)

What to do

- Put a pile of dressing-up clothes on the floor and an empty suitcase.
- Children sit around the clothes in a circle.
- Explain that we're packing for a holiday, and learn/recap the TL names of the items of clothing.
- Child 1 picks up an item of clothing and says its name, placing it in the box/suitcase.
- Child 2 picks an item, says the name of the last child's chosen item followed by their own, places it in the suitcase, and so on ... repeating the whole list of clothing each time.
- If someone forgets an item from the list, they're out.

Variation

The clothes all start off in the suitcase: one by one the children open the suitcase, take out an item of clothing, say what it's called and put it on, then act out an action/activity they could do in that item of clothing. Continue until everyone has had a go/the suitcase is empty

Cross·curriculum link

Drama

Colour by numbers

In my experience children of all ages love the trance-like relaxation of colouring in – this activity is very popular.

Learning objectives

L3.1, L3.3
L4.4
L5.3

Aim

To practise the names of colours and recognise them in written form

Vocabulary

Colours

Resources

- Colouring-in book
- Colouring pens/pencils

What to do

- Give each child a page taken from the colouring-in book.
- Instruct them to draw a grid at the bottom of the page with ten TL colours and to number each colour (see example below).

1 = rouge	3 = vert	5 = noir	7 = marron	9 = rose
2 = bleu	4 = jaune	6 = blanc	8 = gris	10 = violet

- Then they write a number in pencil inside each section of the black-and-white drawing corresponding to the colour they think that section should be.
- Each child then swaps with a friend and completes the colouring-by-numbers activity.

Variation

Older children will enjoy the challenge of looking up more interesting colours in the dictionary, such as 'navy blue', 'khaki', 'turquoise', etc.

Cross-curriculum link

Art

Colour race

A quick game for practising colours

Learning Objectives

O3.2
O4.2

Aim

To recognise the names of colours

Vocabulary

Colours

Resources

- Selection of coloured pencils

What to do

- Children sit in a circle.
- The teacher places pencils one by one in the centre of the circle, saying the TL colours as you go
- When all the pencils are laid out, the teacher calls out a colour and the children must try to beat each other to pick up a correctly coloured pencil.
- Keep going until all the pencils have been picked up; the child with the most pencils at the end is the winner.

Variation

Ask a child to stand at the front of the class with the coloured pencils clutched behind his/her back. As soon as they bring one pencil out in front, the rest of the class must say the correct colour in TL. Whoever says it correctly first gets the next go.

Elodie's colour game

A team game for practising colours

Learning Objectives

03.2
04.2

Aim

To recognise the names of colours.

Vocabulary

Colours

Resources

- Set of coloured cards/sheets stuck to the wall/board or
- Whiteboard screen divided into sections, each section filled in with a different colour

What to do

- Divide the class into two teams.
- A child from each team comes up to the board.
- Say the name of a colour in TL – the first child to touch the correct colour card/section of the board wins a point for their team.
- The two players return to their seats and two more children approach the board.
- After a set amount of time has passed the team with the most points wins.

Magazine scavenger hunt

This cutting-out game can be used to recap many different vocabulary areas, but works particularly well with colours.

Learning objectives

O3.2, O3.4

O4.2

Aim

To recognise the names of different colours and respond.

Vocabulary

Colours

Resources

- Old magazines with colour pictures
- Scissors

What to do

- Give each child a magazine and a pair of scissors.
- One by one, children put up their hand and say the TL name of a colour.
- The rest of the group must try to find and cut out an item in this colour, as quickly as possible, holding it up in the air when they have finished.

Variations

- To make it competitive, award a point to the first child to successfully find and cut out each item.
- Alternatively, older children can give each other a list of items to find and the first one to cut out everything on their list is the winner.
- There are many other ways of varying this game; for example, children have to cut out a picture of something whose TL name begins with a particular letter of the alphabet.
- You could then use the pictures to make a collage or as the basis of a wall-display.

Cross·curriculum link

Art

Set your sights

This simple game is great for practising colours – and other vocabulary areas too.

Learning objectives

03.2, 03.4

04.2

Aim

To recognise the names of colours and practise saying them.

Vocabulary

Colours, numbers

Resources

- Sheets of A4 paper in different colours
- Two beanbags

What to do

- Divide the group into two teams, sitting in a line at opposite ends of the room.
- Lay the sheets of A4 coloured paper out on the floor.
- One by one, a child from each team comes forward and must throw a beanbag on to a sheet and correctly name the TL colour.
- A point is given for each correct answer.
- If the beanbag lands in between two sheets, a player from the opposing team may give the name of a colour in English which their opponent has to say in TL.
- Children are not allowed to aim for the same colour as the child whose turn immediately preceded theirs!

Variations

- This game can also be used to practise animals, foods, or just about any vocabulary area for which you have a set of A4 picture cards (simple drawings are fine or print images from a computer).
- Or you could print off a set of flags of the different countries where the TL is spoken and children have to name the country on whose flag their beanbag lands.
- For older children practising numbers, write numbers between 1 and 100 or even 1,000 on paper plates. Turn over all the plates and only reveal the number when the player has thrown their beanbag on to it.
- For older children who have mastered their numbers, write simple maths problems on the plates – they must give the answer in TL.

Cross-curriculum link

Maths

Country couples

A fun way of advancing geographical knowledge of the countries where your chosen TL is spoken.

Learning objectives

L3.1, IU3.2
04.4, L4.3
05.1, 05.2, 05.3

Aim

To match up the names of countries with their capital cities.

Vocabulary

French/Spanish/German speaking countries and their capital cities

Resources

- Roll of large white stickers
- Two different coloured marker pens

What to do

- Before the lesson begins, write the names of 15 countries where the TL is spoken on to one set of stickers using one of the marker pens. (This number of stickers is for a class of 30 – obviously make more or less stickers depending on the size of the group.)
- Using the other colour, write each country's capital city on to another set of stickers.
- As the children enter the room, stick a sticker on to each child's back.
- The children must find out which country they are and pair up with their capital city – however, they can achieve this only by asking questions in TL to which the answer is 'Yes' or 'No': e.g. 'Am I in Europe?' 'Have I got a famous building?'

Variations

- There are several different things you can write on the second set of stickers depending on what you have been covering in class. For example, instead of capital cities you could write nationalities in TL so children have to pair up e.g. *la Belgique* with *belge*.
- If the children are older and have an advanced knowledge of the different countries you could write the name of a famous person or product from each country.

Cross-curriculum link

Geography

Jumbled earth

A good way to introduce children to the countries of the world that speak their TL

Learning objectives

L3.1, L3.2, IU3.2

L4.3

Aim

To recreate the names of countries out of jumbled bits.

Vocabulary

Countries (see the list of French, German and Spanish speaking countries on page 302)

Resources

- Two sets of 12 country names in TL, written on to strips of card and cut into segments of two to four letters

What to do

- Divide the class into two teams.
- Give each team a set of chopped-up country names which they have to reassemble.
- Tell the teams they have 5 minutes to reassemble all the words
- Start the clock!
- After 5 minutes, ask the children to stop and take turns reading out the country names they have managed to recreate.

Variations

- Children can make the card strips and cut them up for each other.
- You can of course use any other vocabulary you wish.
- As an extension activity, see how many of the countries the children can locate on a map of the world.

Cross-curriculum link

Geography

Round the world trip

Go on an exotic holiday without leaving the classroom!

Learning objectives

03.2, 03.3

04.1, 04.2

Aim

To practise saying and understanding modes of transport and the names of countries where the TL is spoken

Vocabulary

Modes of transport, TL countries

Resources

- A4 cards, each with the name of a country where your chosen TL is spoken

What to do

- Place country name cards around the room.
- Recap (or learn if not previously learnt) the names of several modes of transport.
- Ask the children to form a group sitting in the centre of the room.
- Point to each child in turn and say 'You're going to (country) by (mode of transport)' e.g. *Tu vas au Maroc en voiture*.
- That child must do a lap around the room, miming the mode of transport you have specified, and finish up by the card of the country you have named.
- Once the child has arrived it's their turn to tell the next child where they must travel to and using what mode of transport.
- Continue like this until all the children have arrived at their destination.

Variation

A quicker version, which is useful as a gap-filler/warm-up game:

- Pin up the country name cards around the room.
- Ask the children to stand in the centre of the room and say one of the country names followed by a mode of transport, using a TL phrase as above, e.g. *Vous allez au Canada par avion*.
- The children must all dash to where this country card is located, miming the correct mode of transport – the last child to arrive is out, as is anyone who goes to the wrong country or uses the wrong mode of transport!
- Keep going until you have only one child left, who is the winner.

Cross-curriculum link

Geography

Blind walk

A listening exercise which requires a bit of space.

Learning Objectives

03.2, 03.3, 03.4

04.2

05.3

Aim

To practise listening to and saying a variety of directions.

Vocabulary

Directions

Resources

- Blindfold

What to do

- Children work in pairs: A and B.
- A wears a blindfold while B, giving verbal instructions in TL, leads A around the room without touching them.

Variations

- For safety reasons, clear as many obstacles as possible out of the way of young children.
- For older children, lay a course out using furniture etc. for them to manoeuvre around.

Pin the tail on the donkey

Another party favourite.

Learning objectives

O3.2, O3.3, O3.4

O4.2

Aim

To practise directions.

Vocabulary

Directions

Resources

- Large picture of a donkey with no tail
- Tail cut out of card
- Blu-Tack
- Blindfold

What to do

- Stick the picture of the donkey to a wall in the classroom.
- Ask for a volunteer to be blindfolded and give them the tail, explaining they have to try to attach it to the correct spot on the donkey.
- Spin them around ten times (all the children count in TL together) and guide them towards the donkey picture.
- The rest of the group help by calling out directions in TL – 'left, right, up, down …'.
- Mark where each child places the tail with a cross and their initials; the child who pins the tail nearest to the right place wins.

Character card score

A fun and original drama activity.

Learning objectives

O3.2, O3.3, L3.1

O4.4, L4.3

O5.1

O6.4

Aim

To learn the names of different personality traits and use them in a drama activity.

Vocabulary

Character traits

Resources

- Pack of cards – numbered cards only (remove kings, queens, jacks and jokers)

What to do

- Write the names of about 10 to 12 character traits on the board in TL.
- Assign each child a characteristic: brave, friendly, mean, stupid …
- Shuffle the cards and let each child pick a card. Ask them to read out in TL the number on their card. This is the 'score' for that child's particular characteristic. For example, if the child has been

assigned 'friendly' and picks a card with number 10, they must take on the character of someone very friendly. If they pick a low score however, e.g. 1, they would act in an unfriendly way.

- The children walk about the room, interacting with each other 'in character', consistent with their card score.
- After a few minutes, each child chooses a different characteristic and takes a new card for a new round of interactions.

Variations

- Younger children will find interacting in anything other than English very difficult unless you explain to them that they must use certain phrases you have been working on (greetings etc). However, if you are keen to give this activity a go, they can still be learning the names of character traits and practising their numbers in TL.
- If your class has learnt a basic role-play script by heart, the children could act it out, changing their attitude according to their character card scores.
- Older children who have a wider vocabulary and better language skills may complete the activity entirely in TL.

Cross-curriculum link

Drama

Emotion jump

Let the frustrated actors in your class improvise a wide range of emotions.

Learning objectives

03.2, 03.3
04.2

Aim

To practise emotion words in an improvisation activity.

Vocabulary

Emotions

What to do

- Seat the children as an audience with a 'stage' area to the front of the class.
- Ask for volunteers and establish a scenario, e.g. a parent and child discussing the child's day at school.
- As the actors improvise and develop the scene (in English), call out an emotion or state of being in TL. The actors must immediately assume that emotion/state and incorporate it into the scene.
- With the audience's help, continue to feed the actors different emotions throughout the scene – either giving one emotion for all the actors to emulate, or providing each actor with a different emotion.
- For a list of example emotions see the vocabulary lists (pages 261, 276 and 291) for your chosen TL.
- Some example scenarios:
  - Sitting on a frozen lake, fishing through a hole.
  - Trying to sleep while neighbours are being noisy.

- Painting a masterpiece.
- Sitting on a crowded bus trying to read someone else's paper.
- A traffic warden writing out a fine.
- A tight-rope walker half way across the Niagara Falls.
- On a bumpy train trying to do some complicated needlework.
- A mountaineer trying to pull a friend up to the top.
- Having coffee when a fly lands in your cup.
- A postman delivering letters to a house with a dangerous dog.
- Having a shower when the phone rings.

Cross-curriculum link

Drama

Emotional masks

Have fun making masks and use them to learn the names of different emotions.

Learning objectives

03.2, 03.3
04.2

Aim

To practise saying and understanding emotion words.

Vocabulary

Emotions

Resources

* Masks depicting different emotions

What to do

* Children take turns to put on one of a collection of masks, each of which depicts a different emotion.
* Make sure that the child wearing the mask does not know which mask he has on – the others call out the emotion being displayed: *fâché!*, *heureux!* etc. – the mask wearer must perform an appropriate action.

Variation

Get the group to make the masks themselves as a class craft activity – use paper plates and elastic, large paper bags or a mask template printed on to card and 20 cm (8 in) lengths of bamboo to hold them up.

Cross-curriculum link

Drama

Musical emotions

Another version of a party game.

Learning objectives

03.2, 03.3

04.2

Aim

To listen and respond to the names of different emotions.

Vocabulary

Emotions

Resources

* CD player and music

What to do

* As the music plays the children dance about the room.
* When you stop the music, call out the name of an emotion in TL.
* The children must freeze into an appropriate expression of that emotion.
* After a few times, pick a different child each time to name an emotion for the rest of the group to emulate.

Variation

For younger children, instead of emotions call out the TL names of animals; the children must freeze in an appropriate stance.

Finger lickin' charades

Children will love acting out eating their favourite foods with relish!

Learning objectives

03.2, 03.3

Aim

To practise the names of foods.

Vocabulary

Foods

What to do

- Children take turns to mime eating a particular food – e.g. peeling a banana and taking a bite; making a sandwich by cutting bread, spreading it with butter and putting slices together ...
- The rest of the group has to guess which food is being mimed and say its name in TL.
- Whoever guesses correctly takes the next turn.

Variation

This simple version of charades can be used to practise many vocabulary areas – children can mime putting on different items of clothing, or using a variety of household/classroom objects ...

Fruity taste·test

Tests children's knowledge of the names of different fruits ... and they get to eat them, too! Check for any allergies first.

Learning objectives

03.2, 03.3

Aim

To recognise different fruits by their taste and to name them.

Vocabulary

Food (fruit)

Resources

- About ten different fruits, cut into cubes
- Paper plates or bowls

What to do

- Place pieces of each fruit on to two plates.
- Divide the class into two teams and blindfold the first player from each team.
- Player 1 takes a piece of fruit from the plate, eats it and must say its name in TL. If correct, they gain a point for their team and pass their blindfold to player 2.
- Repeat with player 1 from the opposite team and continue until everyone has had a go.

Variation

To make this game non-competitive divide the class into pairs. The two children take turns to wear the blindfold and eat all ten pieces of fruit, naming them one by one, as their partner ticks them off a list. Then swap – see who has got most fruit names correct.

My grandmother went to market

A memory game.

Learning objectives

03.2, 03.3

04.1

Aim

To listen to and repeat a variety of vocabulary.

Vocabulary

Food, any

What to do

- Children sit in a circle.
- Teach the children an appropriate TL phrase, e.g. *Ma grandmère est allée au marché, elle y a acheté ...*
- The first child repeats the phrase, giving the name of a food (or other object) that you have learnt as a class: *Ma grandmère est allée au marché, elle y a acheté UNE POMME.*
- The next child must repeat the phrase with the last child's object and add one of their own: *Ma grandmère est allée au marché, elle y a acheté UNE POMME et DU PAIN.*
- Continue like this around the circle with the list getting longer and longer.
- Whoever muddles up the list or forgets an object is out!

Variations

- You can simplify this for very young children by missing out the 'My grandmother went to market ...' part and have each child just give the name of a food or object by itself.
- Be creative and make the phrase repeated by each child relevant – e.g. if it is clothes you want to practise then your phrase could be 'Ma grandmère est allée en vacances, elle a mis dans sa valise ...'

Shopping lists

> The more this activity mimics a real shopping experience, the better.

Learning objectives

O3.2, O3.3, L3.3

O4.1, O4.2, L4.4

O5.1

O6.2

Aim

To practise food vocabulary.

Vocabulary

Food (greetings and shopping phrases)

Resources

- Plastic food items
- Paper and pens

What to do

- Before beginning, the children each write a shopping list in TL of ten food items.
- Children sit in a circle with the plastic foods in the centre.
- Swap shopping lists across the circle.
- Nominate two children; child A has to ask B for each item on their list in turn; B must collect the items from the pile and hand over to A.
- Nominate a new A and B.

Variations

- If you have time this activity is perfect for role-play. Set up a shop using a table as the counter and place the food items on it. Child A enters with a shopping list and asks for the items while B plays the role of the shopkeeper. This enables children to practise greetings and other phrases associated with shopping ('Hello/Goodbye', 'Please/Thank you', 'Please may I have ...', 'How much', etc.).

- If you can get hold of some plastic euro coins and notes this will provide an excellent introduction to the monetary system of many European countries – discuss the coins, how many cents in a euro, how much a euro is worth, etc.

Cross-curriculum link

Drama

Age walk

> This role-play listening exercise requires children to recognise numbers in conjunction with the basic phrase 'I am … years old'

Learning objectives

03.1, 03.2, 03.4

04.2

Aim

To listen to and recognise numbers in a simple sentence format and respond accordingly.

Vocabulary

Numbers, greetings

What to do

- Children spread out around the room, each occupying their own space.
- Call out an age using the appropriate phrase the children have learnt (for example, *J'ai trois ans*).
- The children must immediately 'become' that age, adjusting how they talk to each other, play, move …
- Give children a minute or two to explore each age before calling out the next.

Variations

- You can call out the ages in sequence to keep it simple, or experiment with giving numbers out of sequence for a more challenging listening exercise.
- The children can take turns calling out ages themselves instead of you.
- This works well even if the children only know numbers up to 10, but with numbers up to 100 children can be very imaginative, role-playing teenagers, adults, people in old age ...
- This activity can get noisy as the children get involved in each role, so you may want to make it a 'miming-only' exercise!

Getting to know you

A gap-filler for practising introductory phrases.

Learning objectives

03.2, 03.3

04.2, 04.4

05.1

Aim

To practise 'introducing yourself' phrases

Vocabulary

Introducing yourself

What to do

- Children walk around the room, shaking hands and using introductory phrases in TL such as: asking/telling each other's names, asking the other person how they are and asking where they live etc.
- After a few moments' practice, stop the children and introduce a setting – examples might be: a reunion party for old friends who have not seen each other for 20 years; a funeral; a library where you are only allowed to whisper; or (not for the faint-hearted) a factory where everyone has to shout above the noise of heavy machinery
- Ask the children to carry on greeting one another in a manner appropriate to the given setting

Cross-curriculum link

Drama

Greetings race

A very quick gap-filler for practising greetings.

Learning objectives

03.2, 03.3

04.2

Aim

To practise greetings.

Vocabulary

Greetings

What to do

- You and the children sit or stand in a circle.
- Explain that you have 'collected' some TL greetings and they are in your pocket – recap two alternative words for either 'Hello' or 'Goodbye' (depending if it is the beginning or the end of the lesson).
- Turn to the child to your left, shake their hand and say the first word for 'hello' (or 'goodbye') e.g. *bonjour*.
- Ask the child to pass it to the child on their left with a handshake, and so on all the way round the circle clockwise.
- Meanwhile shake hands with the child on your right and say the other TL greeting (e.g. *salut*) and ask them to pass it on anti-clockwise.
- See which greeting 'arrives' back in your hand first – when they have both 'arrived' put them back in your pocket safely for next time.
- Note that the child halfway round the circle at the cross-over point will have the tricky task of passing on both greetings at the same time and must concentrate hard not to get them muddled up!

Identity parade

A fun question-and-answer activity.

Learning objectives

O3.2, O3.3

O4.1, O4.2, O4.4

Aim

To practise basic greeting phrases.

Vocabulary

Greeting phrases

What to do

- Each child chooses a TL name, town and age which they must write down but keep secret (e.g. *Michel*, *Paris*, *huit ans*) Then the children stand in a line.
- One child is the police interrogator and walks along the line before asking a 'suspect' child *Comment t'appelles-tu?*
- The child being asked must answer the question, giving either their real chosen name or bluffing, i.e. giving another's name.
- If the interrogator senses the suspect is lying, the interrogator says so (*Tu es menteur!* etc.); the suspect must then own up if the accusation was justified – if so, they sit down and the interrogator goes on to question another suspect.
- If the interrogator is satisfied that the truth is being told, they continue to question the same child (*Quel âge as-tu?*, *Où habites-tu?*) – if the child is in fact lying, then they have got away with it!
- At any point while being questioned the suspect can lie, and at any point the interrogator can accuse a suspect of lying.
- If a child is falsely accused of lying, the suspect replaces the interrogator.

Cross-curriculum link

Drama

Musical greetings

Another version of a party game.

Learning objectives

O3.2, O3.3, O3.4

O4.2, O4.4

Aim

To practise greetings.

Vocabulary

Greetings

Resources

• CD player and music

What to do

• As the music plays, the children walk about the room.
• When the music stops, they must each find a partner and greet them with TL phrases they have learnt: 'How are you?', 'What is your name?', 'How old are you?' ... etc.
• The last pair to complete the task each time is out.

Pass the ball

A quick way to practise questions and answers.

Learning objectives

O3.2, O3.3

O4.2, O4.4

Aim

To practise questions and answers

Vocabulary

Introducing yourself

Resources

- Tennis ball
- TL name badges (optional)

What to do

- Children stand in a circle.
- Child 1 begins by throwing the ball to another child across the circle – as they throw the ball they ask a TL question e.g. 'What is your name?'
- As child 2 catches the ball they answer: 'My name is …' then throws the ball to child 3 … and so on until all the children have asked and answered a question.

Variations

- Use this activity in the early stages of learning to practise one question and answer at a time as you learn them, or later on to practise all the 'introducing yourself' phrases at once, with each child choosing which question they ask, e.g. 'What is your name?', 'How old are you?', 'Where do you live?'... etc.
- For younger children for whom accurately throwing and catching a ball may be difficult (or dangerous!), or if you don't have much space, sit the children in a circle and have them roll the ball across the floor to each other.

Squeak, piggy, squeak

A party game young children love.

Learning objectives

O3.1, O3.2, O3.3, O3.4

O4.2, O4.4

Aim

To practise counting and asking/giving names.

Vocabulary

Numbers one to ten, greetings

Resources

- Scarf or similar to use as a blindfold

What to do

- Children form a circle around a blindfolded player.
- Everyone in the circle holds hands and walks round to their right, counting to ten in TL.
- Once they have reached ten, the blindfolded child holds out their arm and points to someone in the circle (without being able to see them) and asks in TL 'What is your name?'
- The child being pointed to must respond with the requisite phrase ('My name is ...') but they may disguise their voice and use the name of another child in the class to trick the child in the middle.
- The blindfolded child has three guesses to correctly identify the 'squealer'; when the guess is correct they swap places.
- If the child pointed to does not want to be blindfolded, allow them to nominate a friend to wear the blindfold and stand in the middle instead.

Where do you live? 1

Increases knowledge of the geography of a particular country.

Learning objectives

O3.2, O3.3, L3.1, IU3.2

O4.2

Aim

To locate correctly major towns on a country map; to practise saying these names and asking/answering the question 'Where do you live?'

Vocabulary

Introducing yourself, town names

Resources

- Large map of France, Germany, Spain or other country where your chosen TL is spoken
- Small cards with the names of some of the country's major towns written on
- Blu-Tack

What to do

- Pin the map up on the wall or board.
- Ask for two volunteers to come up to the map.
- Hand child 1 a town name card with a piece of Blu-Tack attached to the back – child 1 must not allow child 2 to see this.
- Child 2 stands with their back to the map as child 1 attaches the town card to the correct location on the map and then goes back to their seat.

- Children take turns to raise their hand and ask child 2 'Where do you live?' in TL.
- Child 2 has three guesses as to which town has been stuck on the map and answers accordingly: 'I live in ...'
- If child 2 guesses the correct town they stay put for a second turn and another child comes up to the board to stick on a town name.
- If unsuccessful, child 2 returns to their seat and another child comes up to the board.

Variation

This activity can easily be transformed into a team game:
- Divide the class into teams, A and B.
- A child from team A goes to the front of the class and stands with their back to the board.
- A child from team B then goes to the map and sticks on one of the town names, which child A cannot see.
- The rest of the class ask child A 'Where do you live?' – child A answers 'I live in ...', guessing which town has been stuck on.
- If correct, it's a point to team A. If wrong, team B gets a point.

Cross-curriculum link

Geography

Where do you live? 2

Increases knowledge of the countries where your chosen TL is spoken.

Learning objectives

O3.2, O3.3, L3.1, IU3.2

O4.2

Aim

To correctly locate countries on a world map; to practise saying their names and asking/answering the question 'Where do you live?'

Vocabulary

Introducing yourself, country names

Resources

- Large map of the world
- Small cards with the flags of some of the countries where the TL is spoken drawn/printed on
- Blu-Tack

What to do

- Pin the map up on the wall or board.
- Ask for two volunteers to come up to the map.
- Hand child 1 a flag with a piece of Blu-tack attached to the back – child 1 must not allow child 2 to see this.
- Child 2 stands with their back to the map as child 1 attaches the flag to the correct location on the map and then goes back to their seat.

- Children take turns to raise their hand and ask child 2 'Where do you live?' in TL.
- Child 2 has three guesses as to which country's flag has been stuck on the map and answers accordingly: 'I live in ...'
- If child 2 guesses the correct country they stay put for a second turn and another child comes up to the board to stick on a flag.
- If unsuccessful, child 2 returns to their seat and another child comes up to the board.

Cross-curriculum link

Geography

Bubblegum

An unusual role-play activity, good for warming up the class.

Learning objectives

O3.1, O3.3

O5.2

Aim

To use phrases of disgust in a role-play.

Vocabulary

Phrases of disgust

What to do

- Everyone sits in a circle.
- The first child begins by chewing an imaginary stick of bubble-gum, then takes it out of their mouth and does something really disgusting with it (rubs it in their hair, sticks it up their nose, etc.).
- This elicits an appropriate TL response from the next child (*C'est dégueulasse!* etc.), who must take the piece of imaginary gum and continue to chew, adding their own horrid action.

Cross-curriculum link

Drama

Orchestra

A relaxing way to round off a class.

Learning objectives

O3.2, O3.3

O4.2

Aim

To learn, listen and respond to the names of musical instruments.

Vocabulary

Musical instruments

Resources

* CD player and classical music

What to do

* Ask the children to sit in a semicircle, like the members of an orchestra.
* Teach the names of a number of musical instruments (see Vocabulary section on pages 264, 279 and 294), imitating how you would play each instrument silently as you say them.
* Play some rousing classical music in the background and, as you call out the names of instruments, the children must mime playing the correct one.

Variation

For a competitive element, anyone miming the wrong instrument is out.

Which room are we in?

An excellent gap-filler if you have a few minutes left at the end of a lesson.

Learning objectives

O3.2, O3.3

Aim

To practise the names of the rooms of the house.

Vocabulary

Rooms of the house

What to do

- Children sit to one end of the room like an audience, facing a 'stage' area.
- One at a time children go 'on stage' and, using only mimed actions and objects, show which room of the house they are in. For example, mime washing up, cooking or making a cup of tea for 'kitchen'.
- The rest of the group raise their hands to guess, using TL, which room the child 'on stage' is pretending to be in.

Cross-curriculum link

Drama

Imaginary Name Volleyball

Giving each child in the class a name from a TL country makes the learning experience more authentic; this game helps children to practise saying the names.

Learning objectives

O3.2, O3.3, IU3.3

Aim

To practise TL names.

Vocabulary

Names

What to do

- Give each child in the group a TL name; as you hand out each name badge, say the name clearly for the group to repeat so they can practise the correct pronunciation.
- Divide the group into two teams.
- Position the teams opposite each other across an imaginary volley-ball net.
- The first server for team 1 hits an imaginary volleyball over the 'net', calling out the name of a player on the opposite team.
- The named player must either hit the 'ball' to a team-mate or back across the net, either way calling out the name of the intended recipient.
- As in real volleyball, only three 'hits' are allowed per side before the ball must cross the net.

It wasn't me!

A fun way to practise TL names and also negatives.

Learning objectives

O3.2, O3.3, IU3.3

O4.1

Aim

To practise TL names and negative phrases.

Vocabulary

TL names

Resources

- TL name badges

What to do

- The class sit in a circle, you among them. Each child wears a TL name badge.
- Make an announcement in simple TL that you have lost something, e.g. *J'ai perdu ma clef*, then accuse one of the children of taking it: *Etienne, tu as pris ma clef?*
- 'Etienne' then denies the accusation using a negative form and accuses someone else: *Je n'ai pas la clef, Sylvie a pris la clef*
- Sylvie denies the accusation using the same formula, and so on ...
- Continue until everyone has had a chance to defend themselves!

Variation

You can make the language used in this activity more or less sophisticated depending on the TL knowledge among your group. For older children try practising phrases using complex pronouns and negatives, e.g. *C'est François qui l'a pris* and *Je n'ai jamais vu la clef*.

Name gestures

This gentle warm-up activity focuses children's concentration.

Learning objectives

03.2, 03.3, 03.4, IU3.3

04.2

Aim

To practise TL names.

Vocabulary

Names

Resources

• TL name badges (optional)

What to do

• Give each child a TL name badge (or just point to each child in turn), saying the names as you give them out so that the children hear the correct pronunciation.
• Standing in a circle, the first child announces their name while performing an accompanying gesture (e.g. shoulder shrug, pirouette, touching toes ...)
• The next player repeats that name and action, then says their own name adding a gesture of their own.
• This continues around the circle until the last child must repeat everyone else's name and gesture before adding their own.

Pass the key

A quiet party-type game.

Learning objectives

O3.2, O3.3, IU3.3

O4.2

Aim

To practise TL names and counting.

Vocabulary

TL names, numbers one to ten

Resources

* TL name badges
* Key on a long circle of string

What to do

* Children sit in a circle, with one child ('it') sitting in the centre
* 'It' closes their eyes and counts slowly to ten in TL.
* Meanwhile, the other players grip the string with both hands and pass the key along it, keeping the key hidden inside their hands at all times.
* When 'it' reaches ten, the children stop passing the key but keep their grip on the string – 'it' opens eyes and tries to guess whose hand the key is in by looking for a guilty face.
* 'It' chooses a suspect and asks '(Name), where is the key?' in TL.

- The suspect opens their hands for all to see. If the suspect does have the key they say 'Here it is'; if they do not then they say 'I don't know' (in TL).
- 'It' must identify who has the key in three attempts, otherwise a new 'it' is elected.
- If 'it' guessed correctly, then the suspect becomes the new 'it'.

Variation

If you do not have a long piece of string, children can simply pass the key from hand to hand and when 'it' opens their eyes, they hold their clenched fists out in front of them.

Occupations

> **A memory activity.**

Learning objectives

O3.2, O3.3

O4.1, O4.2

Aim

To correctly use phrases incorporating the names of occupations.

Vocabulary

Occupations, TL names

Resources

- TL name badges

What to do

- Before you start, you may need to recap the names of occupations in TL.
- Children sit in a circle.
- Child 1 introduces himself and gives an occupation: *Je m'appelle Henri et je suis professeur.*
- Child 2 repeats this information, then introduces herself: *Il s'appelle Henri et il est professeur, je m'appelle Lucille et je suis médecin.*
- Continue around the circle with each child adding their occupation to the list until everyone has introduced themselves.

What's my line?

A fun drama activity based on the famous party game.

Learning objectives

O3.3, L3.1

O4.2

Aim

To practise the names of occupations, asking questions.

Vocabulary

Occupations

Resources

- Cards with pictures of people in a variety of occupations/names of occupations in TL

What to do

- Prepare a selection of cards with pictures/names of occupations in TL (gardener, ballet dancer, jockey, secretary, astronaut, policeman …)
- Ask the first child to pick a card; the others sit in a circle while child 1 mimes what is on the card.
- Children are not allowed to speak or give any clues.
- The rest of the group must guess the job; the child who guesses correctly chooses the next card.

Variations

- Give each child a wooden brick/cuboid box and cover with white paper. On each side draw a person dressed for and carrying out a different occupation. Children take turns to roll the dice and act out the occupation for the other children to guess.
- Instead of drawing pictures, write the TL words for occupations on the dice for reading practice

Cross-curriculum links

Drama, art

Big and small

A few ideas for practising 'big' and 'small' words with young children.

Learning objectives

O3.1, O3.2, O3.3

Aim

To practise using size words.

Vocabulary

Size

Resources

* Pairs of household objects that are identical or similar except for their size (teaspoon/serving spoon; large teddy/small teddy; adult shoe/doll's shoe ...)

What to do

* Place the objects in the centre of the circle.
* Begin by holding up the objects one by one and saying 'big' or 'small' in TL, asking the children to repeat.
* Ask each child to pick an object from the centre and say in TL whether it is 'big' or 'small'.
* Go around the circle, asking each child to say 'big' or 'small' to the child on their left, who must then pick out an appropriate object from the centre and hold it up.

- Introduce the words for 'tiny', 'enormous' …
- One by one ask the children to stand up; ask another child in the group to say a size word, upon which the child standing must either stretch out to make their body as big as possible, or curl up tiny on the floor.

Variation

See page 244 for a rhyme for young children using size words: 'A little cake, a bigger cake …'.

Concept matching

A simple, quiet activity for young children.

Learning objectives

03.2, 03.3

04.2

Aim

To recognise characteristics of a variety of objects.

Vocabulary

Size, shape, colour ...

Resources

* Household objects or pictures

What to do

* Using real objects (household implements, Russian dolls) or pictures of animals, vehicles, etc. ask children to say in TL whether an object is small or large, or tiny, minute, enormous, gigantic ...
* Which of the items is red, blue, green ...? Soft, hard, long, round, straight, floppy ...?

Cross-curriculum link

Science

Odd one out

A sorting game.

Learning objectives

O3.3, O3.4

O5.1

Aim

To recognise which category different objects belong to and why.

Vocabulary

Classroom/household objects, animals, foods ...; negatives

Resources

- Variety of objects, pictures, etc.

What to do

- Arrange objects or pictures on a table, or in the centre of a circle of children, where they can easily be seen. Ensure at least one does not fit into the category of the others (e.g. have a selection of plastic fruit and one pen).
- Ask the children to decide which is the 'odd one out' and tell you why in TL. Encourage them to use negative phrases: 'Because it's not a ... (food, animal)'.
- Ask children to take turns to rearrange the objects/pictures, leaving an 'odd one out' each time, and ask their classmates which one is 'odd' and why.

Birthday dash

> Younger children may need a little help remembering which month their birthday is in!

Learning objectives

03.2, 03.3

04.2

Aim

To understand and respond to the months of the year.

Vocabulary

Months of the year

What to do

- Children stand in a circle.
- Begin slowly chanting the months of the year in TL.
- Each child must listen out for the month of their birthday; when it is chanted they must run across the circle to a space on the other side.
- Anyone who bumps into another child, doesn't run when their birthday month is mentioned or runs at the wrong time is out.
- Repeat two or three times.

Variation

For older children, when the month of their birthday is chanted they must run across the circle shouting the date of their birthday in TL, e.g. '15th of October!'

Dressing up

This activity really encourages creative language use.

Learning objectives

O3.3

O4.1, O4.2, O4.4

IU5.1, IU5.2, IU5.3

Aim

To use clothes to practise vocabulary and explore differences between countries/cultures.

Vocabulary

Clothes, weather, politeness phrases, numbers ...

Resources

• Selection of dressing-up clothing

What to do

• Have the children dress up as for a particular kind of weather, a familiar location or event (going on holiday, going to school, bedtime...)
• A child who is dressed up can describe in TL the weather they are dressed for, say where they are going, say what time it is ...
• Alternatively, the rest of the group can put up their hands to try to guess in TL what weather/event/time the child is dressed up for.
• Or, if your group is small enough, have a pile of clothes in the centre of a circle and then simply say a type of weather (e.g. *Il pleut*) or an event/place (e.g. *Nous allons à la plage*) and let the children dress up accordingly.

Variation

With a few clothes the possibilities for TL situations are more or less endless. For example, use them to talk about how people dress in the different countries where your chosen TL is spoken.

Cross-curriculum link

Geography

Weather guess

Another simple miming activity.

Learning objectives

O3.3

O4.1

Aim

To practise weather phrases.

Vocabulary

Weather

Resources

- Outdoor clothing (optional)

What to do

- One at a time, children mime getting dressed up to go out in a certain type of weather.
- Alternatively, children can mime how they would act if they had just got in from outside where it is raining/hot/windy.
- The rest of the group must guess the weather in TL, e.g. 'It's raining'.

Variation

If you do have some dressing-up clothes handy this will really enhance the fun of this activity – useful items include a hat, scarf and gloves; overcoat; sunglasses; Wellington boots; umbrella

Cross-curriculum link

Drama

What time is it?

A crazy but fun way of practising telling the time.

Learning objectives

O3.2, O3.3

O4.2

Aim

To practise telling the time.

Vocabulary

Telling the time

Resources

- Four large cards with the numbers 3, 6, 9 and 12, written in big writing

What to do

- Children sit in a circle – four children equally spaced around the circle each hold one of the A4 number cards as on a clock face.
- Choose two children (A and B) to go first.
- A third child (C) says a time in TL, e.g. 'half past three'.
- A and B take on the role of the minute hand and the hour hand respectively, and, using the circle of children as the 'clock', must lie on the floor in the correct position to tell the given time. (To distinguish between minute and hour hand, 'minute' can lie with arms stretched above head while 'hour' can keep arms tucked by side.)
- Choose three more children to be A, B and C.

Variation

Once the children have got the hang of this, perform the activity the other way round – two children go off to a corner of the room to decide secretly on a time, then come back to the circle and lie in the shape of the minute and hour hands. The rest of the group must guess in TL what time is being displayed on the 'clock'

Cross-curriculum link

Maths

Practising vocabulary on many different topics

Back·to·back drawing

This quiet, concentrated activity is an interesting way of encouraging careful listening.

Learning objectives

O3.2, O3.3

O4.2

Aim

To listen effectively to your partner and recreate what they have drawn and described.

Vocabulary

Colours, objects, animals, body parts ...

Resources

- Plain paper
- Pens/pencils

What to do

- In pairs, children sit back-to-back (on chairs or the floor).
- Each child has a sheet of paper and some coloured pens/crayons.
- The first child draws while describing in TL the pictures/shapes to their partner, e.g. 'red square', 'blue dog', etc., which the partner must reproduce.
- Compare at the end to see who has been listening most closely.

Cross·curriculum link

Art

Categories

A sorting game for young children.

Learning objectives

O3.2, O3.3

O4.2

Aim

To recognise to which category different objects belong.

Vocabulary

Classroom/household objects, foods ...

Resources

- Variety of objects
- Bags or boxes

What to do

- Arrange a large variety of objects on the floor.
- Give each child a bag or box.
- Give the children the name of a colour in TL and ask them to pick all the objects of that colour and place them in their bag.
- Next give them a category (e.g. fruit, things you would find in the classroom) and ask them to pick out the objects of that type, giving their names in TL as they pick them.

Changing object mime

A simple but focusing drama activity.

Learning objectives

03.2, 03.3

04.2

05.1

Aim

To mime using different objects and say what they are.

Vocabulary

Classroom/household objects, foods ...

What to do

- Sitting or standing in a circle, 'pass' an imaginary object to the child on your right explaining what it is in TL – e.g. *C'est un téléphone*.
- The child must 'take' the object from you and mime with it for a moment before changing it into something else, saying in TL what that new object is, and passing it to the child on their right – the next person must mime the new object, then change it before passing it on ... and so on.

Cross-curriculum link

Drama

Charades

Use this old favourite party game to practise a wide variety of vocabulary areas.

Learning objectives

03.2, 03.3

04.2, 04.3

Aim

To practise a wide variety of words in a guessing game.

Vocabulary

Food, countries, clothing, animals …

What to do

- Once you have agreed the rules of this well-known game with your class, you can play it over and over again to practise different areas of vocabulary. Agree an action for each category and write the categories on the board in TL as a reminder (e.g. food – shovel invisible food into your mouth; country – place your hand over your eyes as if looking at a view; animal – hands up to top of your head like ears …).
- The first actor stands at the front of the room and mentally chooses a TL word which is known to the whole class.
- First the actor indicates a category by performing the correct action. When someone identifies the category, they call it out in TL and, if correct, the actor places their finger on the tip of their nose and points at them.
- Next, the actor indicates how many syllables the word has by placing the requisite number of fingers of their right hand against their left upper arm.

- Next, the actor acts out the word they have chosen – they can indicate that the word 'sounds like' another by tugging their ear.
- Class members raise their hands to guess the answer – whoever guesses the word correctly is the next actor.

Cross-curriculum link

Drama

Chinese relay

This game involves relay running and listening, and requires accurate repetition.

Learning objectives

03.2, 03.3

04.2, 04.3

05.1

Aim

To listen to and repeat accurately words/phrases in a relay-running game.

Vocabulary

Any

What to do

- Divide group into two teams which line up facing each other at opposite ends of the room.
- Whisper the same TL word/phrase to the child at the head of each team line (the leader) then, when everyone is ready, shout 'Ready, steady, go!' in TL
- The leader of each team runs to the opposite wall and back again to whisper the message to number 2 in their team. Number 2 runs across the room and back, passes the message to number 3, etc.
- The game is won when the last person from one team arrives back in position and yells out the word. If the word is correct, that team is the winner. If not, begin again with another word!

Cross-curriculum link

PE

Chinese whispers

A well-known game which can be surprisingly versatile.

Learning objectives

O3.2, O3.3, O3.4, L3.1, L3.2, L3.3

O4.2, O4.3, L4.3, L4.4

Aim

To practise speaking and understanding words.

Vocabulary

Any

What to do

- Children sit in a circle.
- Explain that they will be whispering a word to each other and must make sure they cannot be heard by anyone else, i.e. they should hide their mouth with their hand and whisper very quietly directly into the other child's ear.
- Child 1 whispers a TL word of their choice from a particular vocabulary area (e.g. the name of a food, animal, part of the body ...) to child 2 sitting on their left.
- Child 2 then passes it on to their left etc. until the message has gone all the way round the circle and reaches the child sitting on child 1's right.
- This last child says out loud what they have heard – compare this with the original TL word whispered by child 1.

Variations

- Sometimes children like to deliberately change the TL word as it is passed around to get bigger laughs at the end – you can make it worth their while to listen and repeat the word more carefully by offering a sticker/housepoint etc. for each child at the end if, say, five words get passed round successfully.
- You can make the activity more challenging for older children by writing a list of TL words/phrases on the board for them to choose from, which all sound very similar – the children then have to be careful to pronounce each word very clearly.
- An even harder version of this game is 'Spelling Chinese whispers':
  - Sitting in a circle, child 1 whispers a TL word to child 2 who must write down what they hear on a piece of paper, which is then passed to child 3.
  - Child 3 whispers what is written on the paper to child 4, who again must write it down and pass it to child 5 … and so on, the children alternating between whispering and writing down what they hear/read.
  - The last child must say out loud what they have heard/read.

Favourite things

Practise simple expressions of like and dislike.

Learning objectives

O3.3, L3.2

O4.2, O4.3

Aim

To recognise the starting letter of a word; to practise key politeness phrases.

Vocabulary

Any

What to do

- Divide children into pairs.
- Child A is given a TL name. The rule is that child A only likes things which begin with the same letter as that name.
- Child B tries to offer child A things, asking *Tu aimes... (les bananes)?* to which the answer is given *Non, merci* until something is offered which starts with the same letter as the TL name – *Oui, s'il te plaît!*
- Swap roles.

Variation

- For a more sophisticated version use a more complicated question and reply format: *Non merci, je n'aime pas la fourchette*; *Oui, s'il te plaît, j'aime l'orange!*
- With young children make this a whole group activity, with one child sitting in the centre of the circle as the others take turns to offer things.

Grenouille

A very silly but fun game for practising new vocabulary and/or sentences.

Learning objectives

O3.2, O3.3

O4.2

O5.1, O5.3

Aim

To practise new vocabulary and sentence construction.

Vocabulary

Any new vocabulary

What to do

- Children sit in a circle with a number of objects in the centre.
- Each child must take a turn constructing a TL sentence that includes the name of one of the objects, but must replace it with the word *grenouille* (or a similar silly word in your chosen TL). For example, if the object the child wants to refer to is a spoon, their sentence might be *'Je mange le petit déjeuner avec une grenouille'*.
- The others must guess which object is being referred to and repeat the whole TL sentence correctly.
- Whoever guesses correctly takes the next turn.

Variations

- Younger children can make up their sentence in English but still practise using a new TL word each time.
- If you are feeling daring, instead of substituting the TL word with *grenouille*, allow the children to blow a raspberry instead – children will, needless to say, find this hilarious.

Hurry, waiter!

A team game.

Learning objectives

O3.2, O3.3

Aim

To recall and practise vocabulary on any given topic under pressure of time.

Vocabulary

Any

Resources

- Paper plates
- Ping-pong (or tennis) balls
- Picture cards

What to do

- Divide the group into two, or more, equal teams.
- Each team chooses a waiter and team members line up behind the waiter in single file, leaving a gap between each child.
- The waiter is given a plastic plate with a ping-pong ball on and a pile of cards with pictures on.
- At the whistle, the waiter weaves in and out between team mates, balancing the ball on the plate like a real waiter, and turning at the end to weave back to the start.

- If the ball is dropped the waiter must pick it up and go back to the start. When the waiter arrives successfully back at the head of the team line, the plate and ball are handed to the next player, who must take the top card from the plate and say what it is in TL. The first waiter then rushes back to the end of the line while the new waiter begins weaving in and out.
- Carry on until the original waiter arrives back at the head of the team - the first team to finish are the winners.

Variation

The cards on the plate can contain whatever you see fit – simple maths equations for the children to work out and give the answer to in TL; or, if you don't have cards, the old waiter could say a TL word which the new waiter has to spell out in the TL alphabet...

Cross-curriculum link

PE

Mega machine

A nice warm-up for a cold day!

Learning objectives

O3.2, O3.3, L3.2

O4.3, L4.3

Aim

To practise pronunciation.

Vocabulary

Any

What to do

- Beforehand, discuss with the children what their favourite TL word is – one that they like the sound of and enjoy saying. Ask all the children to choose a favourite word, each one different.
- Clear the room and ask the children to congregate to one side.
- Explain to the children that, as a class, you are going to collaborate together to make one huge machine.
- One child begins by performing a simple repetitive, robot-like action (such as pumping a fist up and down, lifting one knee, twisting from side to side ...) while repeating their favourite word in rhythm with their movement.
- A second child joins them to become part of the 'machine', performing another action along with their word, in time with the rhythm set by the first child.
- Continue until all the children have joined in to make a fascinating machine.

Cross·curriculum link

PE

Memory tray

A popular and simple memory game, also known as 'Kim's game'.

Learning objectives

O3.2, O3.3

Aim

To remember and repeat the names of a variety of objects.

Vocabulary

Food, classroom objects, any

Resources

- Variety of objects
- Tray
- Towel or cloth

What to do

- Children sit in a circle.
- Place ten objects on the tray, and place the tray in the centre of the circle.
- Teach the names of all the objects in TL and reinforce through repetition.
- Explain to the children that they must take a good look at the objects and try to remember what they are.
- Cover the tray with a towel/cloth. How many object names can each child remember?

Variation

An easier version for young children: once they have had a good look at the tray, blindfold one of the children and ask another to remove one object from the tray and hide it in their lap. Remove the blindfold and ask the child who wore it to name the missing object.

Musical fingers

A simple version of a party game.

Learning objectives

O3.2, O3.3

Aim

To listen and respond to vocabulary.

Vocabulary

Any

Resources

- Variety of objects
- CD player and music

What to do

- Children stand in a circle.
- Place a number of objects in the centre of the circle.
- As the music plays, the children walk round in a circle.
- When you stop the music, call out the TL name of one of the objects – the children all have to point at the correct one.
- The last one to point, or anyone pointing to the wrong object, is out.

Variation

If the children know the words to any TL songs then use them - they can sing along as they walk around in a circle.

Pass the parcel

> Another calm but fun party game.

Learning objectives

O3.2, O3.3

O4.2, L4.1

Aim

To practise vocabulary and/or questions and answers.

Vocabulary

Any

Resources

- Simple gift (e.g. pack of pencils/erasers, notebook …) wrapped in brightly coloured gift-wrap
- Newspaper
- Small pictures, objects or cards with TL questions on
- CD player and music

What to do

- Beforehand, wrap the gift in several layers of the newspaper, placing a small object, picture of an object or question card inside each layer.
- Children sit in a circle.
- As the music plays, children pass the parcel around the circle.
- When the music stops, the child who is holding the parcel takes off one layer and must give the TL name for the object or picture, or answer the TL question.
- When the last layer of newspaper has been removed, the child who is holding the brightly wrapped gift when the music next stops gets to unwrap and keep the gift.

Silly soup

A memory activity for practising almost any vocabulary area – it is 'silly' because the things that go into the soup don't necessarily have to be edible!

Learning objectives

03.3

04.1

Aim

To practise vocabulary and remember lists of words.

Vocabulary

Any, household objects, food

Resources

- Collection of objects, e.g. plastic food
- Large pan, bowl or box

What to do

- Children sit in a circle.
- Place the pan in the centre of the circle with the food or other objects next to it.
- Recap the TL names of the foods/objects.
- Ask in TL: 'What shall we put in the soup?'

French	*Qu'est-ce qu'on met dans la soupe?*
German	*Was sollen wir in die Suppe einsetzen?*
Spanish	*¿Qué poner en la sopa?*

- Children raise hands to name a food/object in TL – they then take it from the pile of objects and put it into the pot.
- After each go, recap the list of foods/objects so far – 'What's in the soup?'

French   *Qu'est-ce qu'il y a dans la soupe?*
German   *Was gibt es in der Suppe?*
Spanish   *¿Qué hay en la sopa?*

- Continue until all the objects have been put into the soup.

Variation

Ask the children what they think the soup will taste like – now might be a good time to practise some expressions of disgust! (See the vocabulary sections on pages 261, 276 and 291.)

Sound effects

A novel approach to practising vocabulary, this activity also hones listening skills!

Learning objectives

O3.3, L3.3

L4.4

L5.2, L5.3

L6.4

Aim

To identify objects by the sound they make and say them in TL.

Vocabulary

Any, household objects, animals

Resources

- Collection of objects that make a noise *or*
- CD of sound effects (and CD player)
- Blindfold

What to do

- On a table place the objects that make a noise (keys; paper – tear/scrunch; exercise book – flick pages; clicking pen; balloon – rub to make it squeak ...).
- In pairs, children take turns to wear the blindfold while their partner makes a noise using one of the objects.
- The blindfolded child has to guess the object and says its name in TL.

Variations

- You can do this activity with the whole class at once by using a tape or CD of sound effects. You can make one yourself: using a tape recorder/dictaphone collect noises from around the home – a tap running, toilet flushing, door slamming ...

- Or borrow a CD of sound effects from the local library – you can often find compilations of the kind of effects used in radio productions (feet crunching on gravel, car engines starting up, etc.) which are useful for older children with better sentence structure and vocabulary knowledge.

- For a literacy exercise, have the children sit with a sheet of paper and ask them to write down in TL what they have heard.

- For younger children, borrow a CD of animal sounds and ask them to identify the animals.

Storytelling

Allows older children to be very creative with the language they have learnt.

Learning objectives

O5.1, O5.3

O6.1, O6.2, O6.3, O6.4

Aim

To create a story incorporating specific objects.

Vocabulary

Any

Resources

- Collection of random objects

What to do

- Place a few objects in the centre of the circle and recap their TL names with the group.
- Ask for a volunteer to assume the role of storyteller.
- The storyteller must make up the first part of a simple story in TL, incorporating one of the objects, either in the manner for which it was designed (e.g. *Aujourd' hui il pleut, alors je mets un chapeau*) or in a more creative and unlikely way (e.g. *Aujourd' hui il pleut, alors je mets une assiette*).
- The role of storyteller passes to the next child, with each object used until they have all been incorporated into the story.
- The story must be complete, with a beginning, middle and end.

Variation

This game can be played with younger children, who make up the body of the story in English but must insert the name of each object in TL.

Cross-curriculum links

Drama, literacy

Strange menu

This activity enables children to use new vocabulary along with basic greetings and politeness phrases, in an imaginative role-play setting.

Learning objectives

O3.2, O3.3, O3.4, IU3.3

O4.2, O4.4, IU4.2

O5.1

Aims

- To practise new vocabulary in role-play.
- To listen to each other and respond accordingly.
- To practise phrases appropriate to a restaurant setting.

Vocabulary

Restaurant, greetings

Resources

- Tray or table
- Selection of objects whose names you want to practise

What to do

- Place a few each of a number of objects on a cloth or tray to one side of the room.
- Half the group seat themselves as if in a restaurant, pretending to look at a menu.

- The other half are waiters and stand by the 'kitchen' until the 'customers' show that they are ready to order by waving or clicking their fingers or by calling *Garçon!*
- Each waiter takes a customer's order in TL (of just one object) then goes off, fetches it, and serves it to the customer. Customers must use *s'il vous plaît* and *merci* when ordering.
- If the correct item is served, the customer thanks the waiter, saying *C'est délicieux!* etc., and can order something else. If it's incorrect, the customer makes a big fuss saying *Non, non, non!* and waving the food away.
- After 5 minutes children swap roles.

Variations

This game can be used to practise many different vocabulary areas. For example, if the children have been learning the names of foods then use real or plastic food items. However, just about anything can be used (this is why the menu is 'strange'!). If you have been learning classroom vocabulary then use items such as pencils, rubbers, exercise books, etc.

Cross-curriculum link

Drama

Touching encounters

A quiet activity, popular with young children who love games where they have to close their eyes – no peeping!

Learning objectives

03.2, 03.3

04.2

Aim

To practise describing things and/or to learn new vocabulary.

Vocabulary

Food, household/classroom objects

Resources

* Box containing a variety of objects

What to do

* Ask child 1 to close their eyes and hand them the box of objects.
* Child 1, with closed eyes, takes out one of the objects, saying in TL whether it's hard, soft, big, small, long, round ...
* Child 1 guesses what the object is, asking in TL 'Is it a...?'
* Move on to child 2 and so on around the group.

Variation

Use this activity for teaching new vocabulary – the objects can be those for which the children do not yet know the TL words; when they have finished describing each object tell them the TL word for it.

Touchy·feely

A simple game that makes a good gap-filler.

Learning objectives

O3.2, O3.3

Aim

To practise vocabulary.

Vocabulary

Food, household/classroom objects

Resources

- Box or bag containing a variety of objects (e.g. plastic fruit and vegetables)
- Scarf or similar to use as a blindfold

What to do

- One by one the children are blindfolded and passed the bag of objects.
- They take out an object and, using touch alone, have to identify what it is in TL.
- The bag is then passed to the next child.

Whisper, normal, shout

A fun warm-up, which gets the vocal apparatus ready for pronouncing those tricky TL sounds!

Learning objectives

03.2, 03.3

04.2

05.1

Aim

To practise vocabulary containing the more difficult phonemes.

Vocabulary

Any

What to do

- Ask the class to suggest TL words or phrases they find particularly difficult to pronounce.
- Direct the class, using TL instructions, to repeat the word/phrase at various volumes (whisper, normal, shout ...)
- Alternatively, using either English or TL instructions (depending on ability), direct the class to repeat the words in different styles: hysterical, sinister, opera, robot, babyish ...

Exploring literacy in the target language

Alphabet run

Encourages children to recall previously learnt vocabulary.

Learning objectives

O3.3, L3.1, L3.2

Aim

To say words beginning with a particular letter of the alphabet.

Vocabulary

Any

What to do

- Children stand in a circle.
- Player 1 runs across the circle calling out a TL word beginning with 'A'.
- As player 1 reaches the other side of the circle, they tap another child on the shoulder – that child must run across the circle calling out a TL word beginning with B ... and so on.
- Any child who takes too long to come up with a word or who can't think of one must sit out.
- Continue until all children have taken a turn.

Cross-curriculum link

PE

Body spelling

A novel way of practising TL spellings.

Learning objectives

O3.2, O3.3, L3.1, L3.3

O4.2

Aim

To practise spelling words.

Vocabulary

Any

What to do

- Divide the class into two teams.
- Team 1 confer to come up with a TL word – the word cannot contain more letters than there are team members in team 2.
- Each member of team 2 must create the shape of one of the letters in the given word with their body and together they spell out the whole word.
- Then it is team 2's turn to come up with a TL word for team 1 to spell out.
- Keep alternating between teams – a team point is given for each word correctly spelled.

Variation

Naturally the better your class knowledge of TL vocabulary the more sophisticated the choice of words can be – older children can try to catch each other out with tricky spellings!

Cross-curriculum links

Drama, PE

Crosswords and wordsearches

A simple paper-and-pencil activity for children of all ages.

Learning objectives

L3.1, L3.3

L4.4

L5.3

Aim

To practise reading and writing individual words.

Vocabulary

Any

Resources

- Paper and pens/pencils

What to do

To make a wordsearch:

- Each child draws a grid approximately 12 squares wide and 12 long
- Going forwards, down and diagonally, they write in ten TL words using one square per letter, making sure they write down the words they have used alongside the grid.
- They fill in the remaining squares with random letters and then give it to a friend to see how many words they can find!

To make a crossword:

- On spare paper the children write out ten TL words and see what letters they have in common.
- Then they write them out in a criss-cross formation going both horizontally and vertically so that each word shares a common letter with another.
- They draw a grid into which the words in their criss-cross shape will fit and fill in with black pen any square that will not contain a letter.
- They make up a clue for each of the ten words and write these out alongside the blank grid.
- Then they give their crossword to a friend to complete!

Finger writing

A simple reading/writing (sort of) activity.

Learning objectives

O3.2, O3.3, L3.1, L3.3

L4.1, L4.3, L4.4

Aim

To practise writing and reading words/phrases.

Vocabulary

Any

What to do

- Divide the class into pairs.
- Child A turns their back.
- Child B writes a TL word/phrase on child A's back with a finger.
- Child A has to guess the word or phrase.
- Swap over.

Variation

Try writing words on the palms of each other's hands – it's more visual and slightly easier.

Guess the sound

A listening activity for children with an established vocabulary.

Learning objectives

O3.2, O3.3
L4.3, L4.4

Aim

To listen and identify the correct word.

Vocabulary

Any

Resources

- Tape/CD of simple sound effects.
- An answer sheet listing three multiple choice TL words for each sound effect (optional)

What to do

- Play a tape of sound effects, such as a telephone ringing, a car engine revving, a door slamming ...
- The children must read out the correct answer from the answer sheet, or simply give the TL word if no sheet.

Variation

- Obtain a CD of animal sound effects from the local library for young children who know some animal names. The children have to raise their hand and say in TL what animal has made each sound.
- Alternatively, as a writing exercise, the children must write down the correct answer themselves.

Hangman

An old favourite which is great when children know their TL alphabet.

Learning objectives

O3.2, L3.1, L3.2, L3.3
L4.4

Aim

To recognise words in written form and spell them correctly.

Vocabulary

Any

Resources

- Blackboard/whiteboard

What to do

- A child thinks of a TL word and draws a dash line for each letter of that word on the board.
- The other children must call out letters of the alphabet one at a time and, if a letter called out appears in the TL word, the child at the board must write it on the correct dash line.
- For each called-out letter of the alphabet that does *not* appear in the word, a portion of a hanging man is drawn – head first, then body, arms, legs and finally the rope and gibbet.
- At any point a child can guess what the word is; if correct that child is next at the board. If the class cannot guess by the time the hangman is complete, the writer thinks up a new word and the game begins again.

I spy

A quick warm-up activity.

Learning objectives

O3.2, O3.3, L3.2

O4.1, O4.2

Aim

To think of words beginning with a particular letter, of a particular colour, etc.

Vocabulary

Classroom objects, colours, alphabet

What to do

- Think of an object in the room that is visible to you and everyone else.
- Recite an appropriate 'I spy ...' phrase in TL, e.g. *J'ai un petit oeil qui voit une petite chose qui commence par X* or *qui est de couleur X.*
- Children raise their hands to suggest objects you may be thinking of.
- The child who guesses correctly takes the next turn.

Variation

- If you have labelled many of the everyday objects in your classroom in TL, as is the case in many classrooms, insist the children's suggested answers are in TL.
- For younger children allow them to suggest objects in English but give the letter of the alphabet or colour in TL.

Cross-curriculum link

Literacy

In the bag

Good vocabulary practice.

Learning objectives

O3.2, O3.3, L3.2

Aim

To recognise which letter words begin with.

Vocabulary

Classroom/household objects, food, any

Resources

- Cloth (or other) bags
- Paper labels and string
- Varied selection of objects

What to do

- Place the objects in the centre of the circle/on a table.
- Give each child a bag with a tag tied to it displaying a letter.
- Each child has to choose three objects whose TL name begins with that letter and place them in the bag.
- The children then take turns showing their objects to each other and saying their names.

Make your own flashcards

These flashcards can be kept and used again as often as you like as a 5-minute gap-filler.

Learning objectives

L3.1, L3.3

L4.3

Aim

To label pictures, read and write words

Vocabulary

Any

Resources

• Paper, pencils/pens

What to do

• Each child divides a sheet of paper into an eight-square grid and draws a simple picture in each box.
• They colour in each picture and label it underneath in TL.
• They cut the grid up into its squares, and cut the name off each square – they then have a set of 'flashcards'.
• Then each child swaps with a partner and sees who can match up their friend's set of flashcards the quickest.
• Once each pair has completed this task, they can read the TL labels to each other.

Cross-curriculum link

Art

Make your own jigsaw

Again, these can be kept and re-used.

Learning objectives

L3.1, L3.3

L4.3

Aim

To read and write words.

Vocabulary

Any

Resources

- Paper
- Pencils/pens
- Card

What to do

- On a sheet of paper, each child writes a few TL words in large letters, writing each word in a different colour.
- They glue this on to card and leave to dry.
- On the reverse of the card, they draw lines to represent ten jigsaw pieces.
- They cut the card out into jigsaw pieces, swap with a friend and see who can complete their friend's jigsaw first.
- Each child in the pair then reads out loud the words on the other's jigsaw.

Cross-curriculum link

Art

Riddles

This is a good way of practising feminine/masculine adjective endings.

Learning objectives

O4.1, O4.2, L4.1, L4.2, L4.3, L4.4

L5.2, L5.3

Aim

To write your own riddle.

Vocabulary

Any

What to do

- Discuss riddle format as a group – what makes a riddle? Usually it is three descriptive statements followed by the question 'Who/what am I?'. For example: *Je suis jaune et noire. Je suis un fruit. Je suis longue. Je suis quoi?* – Answer: *Une banane.*
- Ask each child to write their own TL riddle, bearing in mind the gender of the object they are describing.
- Have each child memorise their own riddle and then say it aloud for the rest of the group to solve.

Cross-curriculum link

Literacy

Scavenger hunt

Requiring some preparation, this game incorporates a simple reading task.

Learning objectives

O3.3, L3.1, L3.2

L4.3

Aim

To practise reading a range of vocabulary.

Resources

- Collection of small objects
- Small paper bags/cups
- Tick-lists of items written in TL

What to do

- Before the class enters, hide a number of small objects around the room – small balls and toys, photos, coins, paper clips, erasers, playing cards, sweets ...
- Each child (or pair of children, to make the game easier) is given a tick-list of the items to be found around the room, a collecting bag/cup and a time limit of 3 minutes.
- Explain that as the children find the hidden objects they must find the correct word in TL on the list and tick off the items one by one.
- Players set off to hunt for their objects; the winner is the child/pair who finds all the items on the list first, or with the most items ticked off the list at the end of the given time limit.
- To check the contents of the winners' bag/cup, ask them to show each item in turn and say the corresponding TL word, using the list to help them.

Scrambled eggs

'Egg-cellent' for practising accurate spelling in the target language!

Learning objectives

L3.1, L3.3
L4.4
L5.3

Aim

To unscramble the words for different foods in TL and rewrite them accurately.

Vocabulary

Food

Resources

- Paper and pens
- Bilingual dictionary (optional)

What to do

- Give each child a sheet of paper and a pen.
- Ask the children to write, down the left-hand side of the page, the names of ten foods in TL with the letters scrambled – suggest they use a dictionary to check spellings.
- The children then swap with a friend and see who can correctly rewrite the ten words fastest!

Variation

Naturally the vocabulary does not have to be food – use this activity to test the children's writing of TL words on any chosen theme.

Scrapbooks

This project can be ongoing throughout the year, with children adding pages as new vocabulary areas are covered.

Learning objectives

L3.3

L4.4

L5.3

Aim

To practise writing a range of vocabulary.

Vocabulary

Any chosen category

Resources

- A scrapbook each
- Old magazines
- Scissors

What to do

- Give the children a category, e.g. food, clothes, animals ...
- Using pictures cut from the magazines, the children stick them into their scrapbook, labelling each page and item in TL.
- Have wordbooks and dictionaries handy for children to look up any new vocabulary.

Cross-curriculum link

Art

Spelling bee

A twist on the famous American idea.

Learning objectives

O3.2, O3.3, L3.1, L3.2, L3.3

O4.2, O4.3, L4.2, L4.3

Aim

To pronounce and spell words correctly.

Vocabulary

Any

Resources

- List of TL words of increasing complexity

What to do

- The teacher (who can be yourself or a nominated child) has a list of TL words of increasing difficulty.
- The other children are lined up in front of the 'teacher'.
- The 'teacher' says the first word on the list.
- The first contestant must repeat the TL word, spell it out then say it again.
- If correct, contestant 1 sits down and the next contestant is given a new word.
- If incorrect, contestant 1 is out and contestant 2 is given the chance to spell the same word.
- The last player left is the winner.

Variations

- With a small group, if a contestant spells a word correctly, the teacher continues to give the same contestant new words until they spell one wrong.
- To make the game more difficult, players must spell words backwards.
- For a team game:
  - Two teams form a line, standing opposite each other.
  - The 'teacher' calls out the first TL word on the list to one of the players.
  - After contestant 1 on team 1 has attempted to spell it, contestant 1 across from them on team 2 must say if it is 'right' or 'wrong'.
  - If contestant 1 from team 2 gives an incorrect judgement (i.e. says 'right' when contestant 1 from team 1 actually got it wrong, or vice versa) then they are out.
  - If the judgement is correct, contestant 1 from team 2 gets the next word to spell. (The speller stays in the game even if they spelt the word incorrectly.)
  - As players drop out, their places are filled by team-mates, so a speller is always standing opposite a caller.
  - The last team with a player still standing is the winning team.

Tongue·twisters

Excellent for practising pronunciation of difficult phoneme sounds characteristic of each TL.

Learning objectives

O3.2, L3.2

O4.1, O4.3, L4.2, L4.3

L5.1, L5.2, L5.3

O6.2, L6.2, L6.3

Aim

To practise difficult vowel and consonant sounds.

What to do

- The internet is a good resource for finding many tongue-twisters in a variety of languages – try to find ones that particularly target consonant and vowel sounds in the TL which are difficult for native English speakers.
- Print them off or photocopy, and read them aloud together or in small groups.
- Older children can have a go at writing their own tongue-twisters using a dictionary to help them find new vocabulary – the great thing about tongue-twisters is that, although they need to be grammatically sound, they do not really need to make sense.
- Give each child a phoneme to concentrate on; here is a reminder of some of the trickier phonemes:
- French: r as in *rouge*
  distinction between u as in *tu* and ou as in *vous*

distinction between the e sound in *pré* and in *prêt*
- German: ch as in *einfach*
  j as in *Junge* (pronounced y)
  w as in *Wagen* (pronounced v)
  v as in *Vogel* (pronounced f)
  z as in *Zucker* (pronounced ts)
- Spanish: c as in *hacer* and z as in *luz* (pronounced th as in 'think')
  r as in *rápido* and rr as in *perro*
  j as in *Juan*
  d as in *cada* (pronounced th as in 'this')
  g as in *agosto*
  ll as in *calle*
  ñ as in *muñeca*

Examples

French: *La roue sur la rue roule; la rue sous la roue reste.*

German: *Am Zehnten Zehnten um zehn Uhr zehn zogen zehn zahme Ziegen zehn Zentner Zucker zum Zoo.*

Spanish: *El perro de San Roque no tiene rabo porque Ramón Ramírez se lo ha robado. Y al perro de Ramón Ramírez ¿quién el rabo le ha robado?*

Word chain

Excellent for encouraging recollection of vocabulary previously learnt but not used for some time.

Learning objectives

O3.2, O3.3, L3.1, L3.2

O4.2, O4.3

Aim

To think quickly of words beginning with a particular letter.

Vocabulary

Any

Resources

- Tennis ball

What to do

- Children stand in a big circle, well spread out.
- Child 1 begins by throwing the ball to another child across the circle while clearly saying a TL word (e.g. *girafe*).
- The child who catches the ball must say a TL word that begins with the *last* letter of the previous word given (e.g. *éléphant*) before throwing the ball to the next person, and so on ...
- If a child takes longer than 5 seconds to think of a word and throw the ball, they are out and must sit down.
- Continue until you have only one child left.

Enhancing the language-learning experience

Actions to song

This dance activity enables children to practise pronunciation of new language.

Learning objectives

O3.1, O3.2, L3.1, L3.2

O4.2, O4.3, L4.2

L5.1

O6.1, O6.2, O6.3, L6.2

Aim

To listen to a song and make up and perform appropriate actions.

Resources

- CD player and song
- Copies of song lyrics

What to do

- Print out the words to a song in TL – this could be a simple action rhyme for younger children or a pop song for older groups.
- Read through and discuss the text as a group – ensure children understand any new vocabulary.
- Make up actions to fit the words, and finish off by singing/dancing through the song.

Cross-curriculum link

PE

Choosing who will be 'it'

Here are a few ways you can use TL to determine who takes the first turn in a game, or who is 'it'

Heads or tails

- To choose between two players, player 1 says in TL whether they predict a coin will land with heads or tails facing up.
- Toss the coin into the air, catch and place it on back of hand. If the coin lands as predicted by player 1, they are 'it'. If not, player 2 gets to start the game.

Which hand is the (coin, pebble, button) in?

- Behind your back, hold a coin, pebble, etc. inside one fist.
- Bring your fists to the front and whichever player correctly guesses in TL which hand is hiding the coin (by saying in TL 'left' or 'right') is 'it'.

Scissors, paper, stone

- To a count of 'one, two, three' in TL two players shake a fist each in front of them.
- On the count of 'three', they must use the hand to make either: scissors (index and middle finger sticking out like two blades), paper (a flat hand held palm down) or stone (keep the hand balled into a fist).
- The effect of these three objects determines who wins: scissors cut paper (scissors win); paper wraps stone (paper wins); stone blunts scissors (stone wins).

High card

Each player chooses a card from a shuffled deck fanned face down saying the value of their card aloud in TL; the child who picks the card with the highest value wins.

High roller

Each player rolls one or two dice, saying aloud in TL the total number they have rolled – the child with the highest score wins.

Odds and evens

- Two players stand facing each other. One is designated 'odd', the other 'even' (say these in TL).
- On a count of 'one, two, three' (again in TL) each player holds one hand up with 0–5 fingers showing.
- Count the total number of fingers shown by both children aloud in TL. If the total finger count is odd, odd goes first …

Counting off

To divide a group into two teams, line up all the children and work along the line counting (aloud and in TL) 'one, two, one, two …'. All the ones make a team and all the twos make a second.

Emotional pronouns

A fantastic, fun way of using drama to introduce and practise tricky grammar.

Learning objectives

O3.2, O3.3, L3.1, L3.2

O4.2

L5.2

O6.3, O6.4

Aims

- To recognise and pronounce correctly the names of emotions.
- To practise correct conjugation of the verb 'to be' with different personal pronouns.
- To introduce and practise the use of adjectives in their various forms (masculine/feminine, plural ...).

Vocabulary

Emotions, personal pronouns

Resources

- Blackboard/whiteboard

What to do

- Write 12 emotions in TL on the board.
- Ask for one or two volunteers to come up to the front to be the actor(s).
- Ask a further child to suggest a daily activity that is easy to mime, e.g. cleaning teeth, driving a car, making a cup of tea ...

- Ask the actor(s) to choose mentally one of the emotions but not to say it out loud.
- The actor(s) then acts out the activity as if they were experiencing the chosen emotion (e.g. cleaning their teeth as if angry, sad, bored ...)
- The rest of the class raise their hands to guess which emotion has been chosen, using a TL sentence incorporating the correct personal pronoun: 'He is angry' or 'They are bored'.
- Ask the actor(s): 'Are you angry/bored?' The actor(s) must respond, again taking care to use the correct pronoun *and* negative if necessary: 'Yes, I am angry' or 'No, we are not bored'.
- Whoever correctly guesses the emotion chosen by the actors takes the next turn.
- Don't forget sometimes to have one actor alone, sometimes more than one, and mix boys and girls, to enable children to practise all pronouns (singular, plural, masculine and feminine).

Faulty fairy stories

Children pick up new vocabulary very quickly when it is presented to them in a familiar context. They will love the fact that they are allowed to shout out in this activity!

Learning objectives

O3.1, O3.2, O3.3

O4.2, IU4.3

Aims

- To recognise key words in a familiar story and respond accordingly.
- To remember and repeat these words.

Vocabulary

Fairy stories, game-playing

Resources

- Copy of a well-known fairy story (a simple version for younger children)

What to do

- Read the fairy story to the children, replacing key pieces of vocabulary that are often repeated with the equivalent in TL. For example, in 'Goldilocks and the three bears', replace *'bear'*, *'bed'*, *'chair'*, *'porridge'* ...
- Put the book to one side and ask the children who can remember the word for *'bear'*, *'house'* ...
- Read the story again, this time pausing when you get to each TL replaced word, so that the children can provide the word for you from memory.
- When the children are familiar with the story, read it to them again and make deliberate mistakes. For example, 'Goldilocks sat down on the small *ours'*. The children must shout 'Wrong!' *(Faux!* etc.) whenever they detect a mistake.

Variation

To turn this activity into a competitive game, give a point to those children who spot the mistake; anyone who shouts out when there is no mistake loses a point. The winner is the child with the most points at the end of the story.

Cross-curriculum link

Literacy

'Favourites' questionnaire

This activity can be kept very simple or turned into a project lasting several lessons.

Learning objectives

IU3.4

O4.4, L4.1, L4.2, L4.3, L4.4, IU4.2

O5.2, O5.3, L5.2, L5.3, IU5.2

Aim

To gather information about each other's favourite things and collate the results.

Resources

- Paper and pens

What to do

- As a whole class activity, formulate a list of ten questions in TL relating to favourite things, e.g. *Quel(le) est ta couleur/ton animal/ton sujet/ton plat préféré(e)?*
- Photocopy the list so that each child has the questions and have them ask questions of each other, or send them off to 'interview' the children in a neighbouring class.
- When all the questionnaires have been completed, you can make a class activity of charting the results in a variety of ways: pie chart, tower chart, etc.
- Discuss the results – in what ways are our favourite things similar to/different from each other's?

Variation

If you have a link with a school overseas, the children can e-mail this questionnaire to a partner class to see whether the answers they get back are different from those given by children at home.

Cross-curriculum link

Maths

Galette des rois

This cake is traditionally served in France on 6 January (Epiphany). Children will love the suspense of finding out who is *le roi*, followed by eating the cake!

Learning objectives

O3.2, O3.3, IU3.3

IU4.1

L6.1

Aim

To experience an authentic French festivity.

Vocabulary

TL names, greetings/politeness phrases, verbs in conjugated forms (if known)

Resources

- Large cake with a small charm, toy or coin hidden inside
- Knife and paper napkins/paper plates to serve
- Paper crown (preferably gold)

What to do

- Give all the children TL names.
- Bring in the cake (*la galette des rois*) and divide into enough slices for each child.
- The youngest person in the room traditionally shouts out which guest gets each slice of cake.
- Serve the cake (ensuring each child thanks you in TL).

- Whoever gets the slice containing the charm (*la fève*) is the king (*le roi*) or queen (*la reine*) and gets to wear a gold crown for the rest of the day.
- The king or queen then chooses his queen or her king by dropping the charm in that person's lap.

Variations

- According to custom, for the rest of the day every action of the royal pair is watched and imitated with mock ceremony by the entire party, who shout, 'The queen drinks', 'The king laughs', or 'The queen drops her napkin'. This would work well with older children who can use full sentences with confidence.
- Find a recipe in French for the *galette des rois* and make one together as a class.
- Have each child in the class design a crown for *le roi/la reine* to wear; the winning design is the one that gets to be made and worn.
- There is a traditional French rhyme that is sung by children on the *Fête des rois* – see page 244.

Cross-curriculum links

Science, art/design, music

Goldilocks and the three bears

Children enjoy the familiarity of the story while learning new vocabulary and TL sounds.

Learning objectives

O3.1, O3.2, O3.3

Aim

To recognise and use vocabulary embedded in a familiar story.

Resources

- 12 sheets of card
- Copy of 'Goldilocks and the three bears' with selected vocabulary replaced by the TL equivalents (if you need written reminders of the words, use removable stickers stuck over the text, so that you can change languages if teaching more than one TL).

What to do

- On the sheets of card, draw each of the three bears, their three chairs, their porridge bowls and their three beds. Each time, make one drawing large, one medium sized and one small.
- Tell the story in English, but replace the words shown on the cards (e.g. 'baby bear', 'big bowl', 'little bear') with their TL translations.
- Use the cards to illustrate the TL words as you say them, and ask the children to repeat them.
- Distribute the cards among the children and retell the story, each child holding up the appropriate card and saying the TL word as you reach that point in the story.

Variations

- If possible, use real props – three different sizes of teddy bears, real spoons, bowls, etc.
- You can of course adapt this activity for any well-known fairy tale.

Cross-curriculum link

Literacy

Grandmother's footsteps

A variation on a well-known playground game.

Learning objectives

L3.2

O4.1

Aim

To learn and recite a short rhyme.

What to do

- Choose a child to be 'it' (see page 209), who stands facing a wall with their back to the other players, who stand in a line at the other end of the room.
- The other players try to sneak up on 'it' and touch them on the shoulder without 'it' turning around and seeing them move.
- Before 'it' can turn around, 'it' must recite a short rhyme in TL (see pages 244–5). However, 'it' can say this quietly so the other players can't hear and don't know when 'it' is about to turn round.
- When 'it' turns round, the other players must freeze. If 'it' spots any player moving, that player has to return to the start.
- Whoever succeeds in tagging 'it' becomes the next 'it'.

Variation

For younger children for whom remembering a rhyme is too difficult, have them count to ten in TL.

Cross-curriculum link

PE

Greeting cards

Create and send a greeting card at any time of the year!

Learning objectives

L3.3, IU3.3, IU3.4

L4.4, IU4.1

L5.2, L5.3

Aim

To create an authentic greeting card.

Vocabulary

Greetings

Resources

- Card, envelopes
- Pencils, pens
- Bilingual dictionary (optional)
- Internet (optional)

What to do

- Discuss as a group what occasion your cards are going to be for – it may be nearly Christmas or Easter or perhaps you want to raise awareness among your class of celebrations around the globe that are celebrated by speakers of your chosen TL (see the section 'World festivals' on page 304).

- Give each child a sheet of card.
- Each child designs and creates a card, including an appropriate TL greeting inside – this can be achieved using a dictionary or the internet ('e-card' websites such as http://greetings.aol.com with an international section may be useful for inspiration).
- Send the cards to your friends, family or to children at a partner school overseas – if the latter, write the school address on the board for children to copy on to the envelopes themselves.
- Alternatively use the cards to create a display.

Cross-curriculum links

Art, geography, cultural/religious studies

Happy families

Based on the popular card game.

Learning objectives

03.2, 03.3

04.2

Aim

To collect 'families' of cards by asking for them in TL.

Vocabulary

Game playing, numbers, food, animals …

Resources

- Set of normal playing cards with all non-numerical cards removed, *or*
- Home-made set of cards depicting foods or animals (four each of nine different foods/animals)

What to do

- The aim is to create 'families' of four cards, e.g. the 8's of hearts, clubs, diamonds and spades would be one 'family' if playing with normal cards, or all the cows, apples, etc. if using your own set.
- All the cards are dealt, players conceal their cards from one other and the player to the dealer's left begins.
- Player 1 asks (in TL) any other player of their choice for a specific card (e.g. *'three of hearts please'* or *'Cow please'*). Player 1 must already hold at least one card of this same family.

- If player 2 holds the card player 1 has asked for, it must be handed over.
- Player 1 says 'Thank you' in TL and continues by asking the same or another player for a further card.
- If player 2 does not have the required card, they say 'No, sorry not at home' (or 'No', if you want to keep it simple) and it is now player 2's turn.
- Completed families of four are placed face down in front of their owner.
- The player with the most families at the end wins the game.
- A player asking for a card must say 'please', and a player receiving a card must say 'thank you'. Anyone who forgets to do this must give back the requested card (if it has been handed over) and the turn passes to the player they were asking.

Hide and seek

This is just one idea: there are endless possibilities for introducing a TL element to all manner of everyday playground games.

Learning objectives

O3.2, O3.3

Aim

To practise counting.

Vocabulary

Numbers

What to do

- One child is 'it', hiding their face and counting in TL to an agreed number (10, 20, 30 ... or however many they can count to) while the other children run and hide.
- As soon as the counter has finished counting they run to find the other children – the first one to be discovered becomes the new 'it'.

Cross-curriculum link

PE

Higher or lower

An easy but absorbing card game.

Learning objectives

O3.2, O3.3

Aim

To guess whether a card will have the same, higher or lower value as the previous.

Vocabulary

Game playing, numbers

Resources

- Pack of playing cards

What to do

- Shuffle the cards and place face down on table.
- Remove the top card and place it face up next to the pack.
- The first child has to guess – using phrases in TL – whether the next card in the pile will be 'higher', 'lower' or 'the same' in value as the one face up.
- The first child then turns the top card over, saying its value out loud in TL – if the guesser was correct, they get to keep the card; if wrong, they place it face up on top of the original card.
- The second child then has to guess whether the next card to be exposed will be higher, lower or the same as this one. The child who holds the most cards once the pack has run out is the winner.

I only speak ...

A toy who speaks and understands only the TL will be greatly cherished by young children.

Learning objectives

03.1, 03.2, 03.3, 03.4

04.2, 04.3, 04.4

Aim

To teach new language content using a toy to whom the children can only speak in TL.

Resources

* Hard-wearing doll, cuddly animal toy or puppet

What to do

* Explain to the children that you have a special friend who would like to meet them, who has come *all* the way from ... (France, Germany, Spain ...).
* Introduce the toy, giving it a TL name the children can easily remember.
* Explain that the toy doesn't speak any English at all and will only understand the children if they speak to it in TL.
* The toy really wants to get to know the children and be their friend, so it will ask them questions (using your voice of course!) like 'What is your name?', 'How old are you?' and 'Where do you live?'
* Pass the toy round the group as it asks them questions, so they can hold the toy and answer it directly.

- Use the toy as much as possible in lessons for teaching new phrases, vocabulary areas, songs ... etc. As the children learn more about the TL, they can talk to the toy more and more, and ask it questions about the country it is from, etc.
- Warning! The children will fall in love with this toy, so make sure it's not going to fall to pieces after a few cuddles, and be very careful not to lose it!
- Ideally find a toy with moving (or at least recognisable) body parts and even removable clothing, so these vocabulary areas can be taught in TL with help from the children's new friend.

Let's cook!

Use a recipe that does not involve too many utensils (thus not creating too much washing-up), and if you don't have access to a kitchen choose a recipe that does not involve cooking at all, e.g. making smoothies, a typical French/Spanish salad or no-bake dessert ...

Learning objectives

L3.1, IU3.2

L4.1, L4.2, IU4.1, IU4.2

L5.1, IU5.1, IU5.2

Aim

To follow a recipe in TL.

Resources

- Simple recipe in TL – enough copies for the whole class working in pairs
- Ingredients
- Cooking utensils
- Aprons, cloths

What to do

- What you choose to make depends very much on what kitchen facilities you have available to you, as well as the age and number of children in your group – however, there are plenty of recipes that do not involve cooking *per se* at all.

- Discuss the recipe as a group – ensure the children understand what the ingredients are, what quantity of each is required and what utensils are needed.
- Have the children work in pairs.

Variations

- If cooking or preparing food at all just isn't an option in your school there is still some mileage in this activity – ask the children to bring in their favourite recipe and, using a dictionary and your help, translate it into TL. The children could then swap recipes with their friends, take them home and make the food with the help of their parents; the results can then be discussed next lesson – or even brought in to be shared around!
- If your class is in contact with a school in a TL country, the children can ask their oversees friends to e-mail them a favourite recipe.
- Use recipes from a range of countries where your chosen TL is spoken to spark discussion about the different foods and produce available in different parts of the world. If you can lay your hands on some of the more interesting foods in specialist shops and bring them in to show the class, so much the better.
- Investigate the foods/recipes used by TL speakers around the world to celebrate at certain times of the year, such as Christmas.

Cross-curriculum links

Design and technology, geography

Multiple-choice quiz

The children will learn an enormous amount about the language and people who speak it by researching this activity.

Learning objectives

IU3.2, IU3.3

L4.4, IU4.1, IU4.2

L5.2, 5.3, IU5.2, IU5.3

L6.4, IU6.2, IU6.3

Aim

To compile a multiple-choice quiz about the TL and to complete each other's quizzes.

Resources

- Internet, library, books from home

What to do

- You can make this as easy or challenging as you like, depending on the age and ability of the children in your class.
- Split the children into groups of four.
- Explain to the class that each group is going to create a quiz for the rest of the class to complete.
- Using the internet and library as resources, the children must come up with a set of 20 questions to do with the chosen TL and the geography, history and culture of the people who speak it.
- For each question, three possible answers must be provided.
- Once the groups have completed their set of 20 multiple-choice questions, have each group swap quizzes with another group and try to complete each other's.
- When each group has completed the quiz they have been given, the group who originally compiled each quiz gives the correct answers.

Variation

- For younger or less able/independent children, make this a class project where you create one quiz all together and set another class the task of completing it.
- For a less time-consuming quiz activity, see 'Crosswords and wordsearches' on page 189.

Cross-curriculum links

Geography, history, social science, music ...

Puppets

A puppet who speaks only the TL is a really great idea for young children; even better, the children can each make their own puppet and give it a TL name.

Aim

To create a puppet to whom the child can only speak in TL.

What to do

Plate puppet

- You will need: two paper plates, glue, coloured pens, staples, wool, cork.
- Stick two paper plates together (eating surfaces facing inwards) leaving a gap in the edge big enough for the child's hand.
- Paint a face, stick or staple on wool hair, add a hat or cork nose ...
- To use, the child slips a hand between the plates.

Finger puppets

- You will need: stiff card, scissors.
- Draw a body without legs on stiff card.
- Make two holes near the base of the body so that the child can poke their fingers through to make the legs.
- The child could make an elephant by having just one hole and poking a finger through for a trunk.

Sock/sleeve puppet

- You will need: old sock or sleeve, buttons or bottle tops, needle, wool.
- An old sock only needs a face made from buttons/bottle tops stitched on with wool; a sleeve simply needs a knot in the end and a pair of eyes.
- If you place your thumb opposite your fingers, you can make its mouth speak.

Plastic bottle puppet

- You will need: old soft drinks bottle, scissors, wool.
- Cut off the top of a large soft drinks bottle so you are left with a tube that can be decorated.
- Add face, hair, hat, ears ...
- The puppet sits on your hand and wrist and bobs up and down as the puppet 'speaks'.

Paper-bag puppet

- You will need: large paper bag, coloured pens or paints.
- Twist the corners of a large paper bag to make ears, and draw or paint on a face.

Glove puppet

- You will need: old sock, cotton wool, rubber band, 4 x 12 inch piece of felt, scissors, wool, needle and thread, buttons, wool, etc. for face.
- Stuff the toe of an old sock with cotton wool, keeping the stuffing in place with a rubber band. It should be loose enough for a child to poke a finger inside.
- Cut off all but the last 7 cm (3 in) of sock.
- Decorate this head with a face, hair, etc.
- Fold a 10 x 30 cm (4 x 12 in) piece of felt in half, top to bottom.
- Sew the sides together, leaving a hole on both sides near the top for the middle finger to poke out on one side and the thumb to poke out on the other.
- Make a small hole in the top fold and poke the sock head through this.
- Stitch into place.
- To play, poke the forefinger into the head and the middle finger and thumb out through the gaps at the side to make arms.

Hinged puppet

- You will need: stiff card, scissors, split pins.
- Cut out and decorate a head, body, arms and legs from stiff card and hinge together with split pins so the parts can be moved.

Shadow puppets

- You will need: stiff card, scissors, sticky tape, lollipop stick, greasproof paper, table lamp.
- Cut out simple animal silhouettes from stiff card and tape a lollipop stick to each one.
- These can be used to illustrate fairy tales or to create sketches/role-plays.
- Use a large sheet of greaseproof paper as a screen, with a table lamp behind to create a shadow.

Cross-curriculum link

Art

Role-play

A good way of consolidating areas of language that the group has recently learnt.

Learning objectives

O3.3

O4.1, L4.1

O5.1

O6.2, O6.4

Aim

To practise a range of language skills.

Resources

- Props and dressing-up clothes
- Simple role-play scripts

What to do

- Set up the classroom as a particular venue, e.g. school, café/restaurant, post office ...
- Use props and costumes where possible.
- Begin with some very simple pre-written scripts in TL and then encourage the children to develop their own spontaneous exchanges.
- Perform these in front of the rest of the group.

Curriculum link

Drama

Shipwreck

A variation of a popular game – it needs as much space as possible.

Learning objectives

03.2, 03.3

04.2

Aim

To listen and respond to commands.

Vocabulary

Commands

What to do

- Children spread out around the room.
- Explain to the children that they will be asked to run around all in the same direction and must respond to the different commands you call out.
- Teach several commands in TL – they can be as basic or as sophisticated as your group's ability will allow.
- Some basic examples are:
  - *arrêtez!*: stop
  - *allez!*: go
  - *en haut!*: up – freeze and put hands in the air
  - *en bas!*: down – crouch down
  - *tournez!*: turn – run in the opposite direction.

Variation

Older children might like the original commands for this game if you can translate them into TL:

- port: run to one end of the room
- starboard: run to the other
- climb the rigging: climbing action on the spot
- boom coming over: lie down on stomach
- scrub the deck: drop to knees and mime scrubbing
- man overboard: get into pairs and clutch each other
- land ahoy!: raise hand to forehead.

Cross-curriculum link

PE

Songs and rhymes

Songs and rhymes are an excellent way to introduce children to new language content; not only are they enjoyable but evidence suggests that words set to music are much easier to recall. More advanced learners will gain a lot from learning songs entirely in the target language but don't forget there are lots of songs in English that can be 'tweaked' to introduce TL concepts to young children.

Learning objectives

O3.1, O3.2, L3.1, L3.2

O4.1, O4.3, L4.1, L4.2, L4.3

O5.3, L5.1

O6.1, O6.2, L6.2, L6.3

Songs

Heads, shoulders, knees and toes

Simply change the parts of the body into TL and sing while doing the actions (conveniently, in French, it still rhymes!).

Heads, shoulders, knees and toes, knees and toes
Heads, shoulders, knees and toes, knees and toes
Eyes and ears and mouth and nose
Heads, shoulders, knees and toes, knees and toes.

French   *La tête, les épaules, les genoux, les pieds*
             La tête, les épaules, les genoux, les pieds
             Les yeux, les oreilles, la bouche et le nez
             La tête, les épaules, les genoux, les pieds.

Spanish: *La cabeza, los hombros, las rodillas, los pies*
             Los ojos, los oídos, la boca, la nariz ...

German: *Kopf, Schultern, Knie und Zehen (Knie und Zehen)*
Kopf, Schultern, Knie und Zehen (Knie und Zehen)
Augen und Ohren und Mund und Nase
Kopf, Schultern, Knie und Zehen (Knie und Zehen).

I can sing a rainbow

Change the colours into TL and have each child hold up a sheet of coloured paper/coloured object when you get to that colour in the song.

Red and yellow and pink and green, orange and purple and blue
I can sing a rainbow, a French/German/Spanish rainbow, sing a rainbow too.

French   *Rouge et jaune et rose et vert, orange et violet et bleu,*
C'est un arc-en-ciel, un arc-en-ciel pour moi!
[children point to themselves]

German   *Rot und gelb und rosa und grün, orange und lila und blau,*
Schöner Regenbogen, Regenbogen, Regenbogen da!

Spanish *Rojo, amarillo y rosa y verde, naranja, morado, azul,*
¡Es un arco iris, un arco iris, un arco iris hoy!

The Hokey-Cokey

This is a bit trickier to translate, but with a bit of creativity you can knock up a singable version. (La Jolie Ronde have recorded a French version – see www.lajolieronde.co.uk – and the lyrics for a Spanish version charmingly entitled *El Hokey Pokey* can be found at http://songsforteaching.com/spanish/wordfiesta/hokeypokeybodyparts.htm)

Put your right arm in, your right arm out, your right arm in and shake it all about
You do the Hokey-Cokey and you turn around, that's what it's all about.

Put your left arm/right/left leg/whole body... in

If you're happy and you know it...

Sing this in English but translate the actions into TL and have the children repeat them back to you as you sing/perform the actions.

If you're happy and you know it *frappe les mains* (children: *frappe les mains*)
If you're happy and you know it *frappe les mains* (children: *frappe les mains*)
If you're happy and you know it and you really want to show it
If you're happy and you know it *frappe les mains* (children: *frappe les mains*).

If you're happy and you know it *tape les pieds/hoche la tête/hausse les épaules* ... etc.

Old MacDonald had a farm

Younger children can sing the chorus in English but the animal names in TL – don't forget, animals make different sounds in different languages! (Visit the following website for a comprehensive list in many languages: **www.eleceng. adelaide.edu.au/Personal/dabbott/animal.html**)

Old MacDonald had a farm, e-i-e-i-o
And on that farm he had a cow, e-i-e-i-o
With a moo-moo here and a moo-moo there
Here a moo, there a moo, everywhere a moo-moo.

Old MacDonald had a farm, e-i-e-i-o
And on that farm he had a ... (pig, duck, chicken ... etc.)

One finger, one thumb, keep moving

Simply translate the body parts into TL but keep the rest in English.

One finger, one thumb, keep moving
One finger, one thumb, keep moving
One finger, one thumb, keep moving
We'll all be merry and bright!

One finger, one thumb, one arm, keep moving
One finger, one thumb, one arm, one leg, keep moving
One finger, one thumb, one arm, one leg, one nod of the head, keep moving ...

Ten green bottles

Change these three words only into TL for very young children, but you could translate the whole thing. It is good fun to act out, with ten children standing in a line and sitting down one by one with each verse.

Ten green bottles standing on the wall
Ten green bottles standing on the wall
And if one green bottle should accidentally fall...
There'd be nine green bottles standing on the wall.

Nine green bottles standing on the wall ...

Ten in the bed

This is like 'Ten green bottles' above, so have ten children sitting or lying in a row on the floor, with the 'little one' repeating a TL phrase equal to 'Roll over!' each time (La Jolie Ronde have recorded a French version of this song – see www.lajolieronde.co.uk).

There were ten in the bed and the little one said
'Roll over, roll over!'
So they all rolled over and one fell out, he hit the floor and gave a shout.

There were nine in the bed ...

Happy birthday

The birthday of each child in your class presents an ideal opportunity for a memorable TL experience, including counting their age and asking them about their presents in TL. Teach the class a version of 'Happy birthday to you' (to the same tune as the English version) in your chosen TL and sing it to the birthday boy/girl.

French: *Joyeux anniversaire,*
          Joyeux anniversaire,
          Joyeux anniversaire .... (name)
          Joyeux anniversaire.

Spanish: *Que los cumplan feliz,*
          Que los cumplan feliz,
          Que los cumplan ... (name)
          Que los cumplan feliz.

German: *Zum Geburtstag viel Glück,*
          zum Geburtstag viel Glück,
          zum Geburtstag, liebe ... (name)
          zum Geburtstag viel Glück.

London Bridge is falling down...

This Spanish version is sung to the same tune as the English. Two children join hands and form an arch. The other children walk under the arch while singing. The two children bring their arms down on the last word, trapping one child. That child and a partner of their choosing then replace the children forming the bridge.

Este puente va a caer, a caer, a caer.
Este puente va a caer sobre éste(a).

J'aime la galette

This is traditionally sung in France at the *Fête des Rois* held on 6 January – see page 304.

J'aime la galette
Savez-vous comment?
Quand elle est bien faite,
Avec du beurre dedans.
Tralalala lalalalère
Tralalala tralalala.

Rhymes

In a dark, dark wood

Recite the rhyme to the children in English first. Speak in a quiet, creepy voice, and then suddenly shout out the last word and they will love it. Then recite it again in TL – they may be able to provide some of the TL vocabulary themselves.

In a dark, dark wood there's a dark, dark house
In the dark dark house there's a dark dark room
In the dark dark room there's a dark dark cupboard
In the dark dark cupboard there's a dark dark box
In the dark dark box there's a ... GHOST!

A little cake, a bigger cake

This is a French action rhyme for young children. Once they've got the hang of it, change the word 'cake' for animals ('bear', 'hedgehog') starting off curled up on the floor and making their bodies slowly grow bigger.

Un p'tit gâteau,
un grand gateau,
un énorme gâteau je vois!
Comptons les gâteaux –
un, deux, trois!

A little cake, (make a fist)
a bigger cake, (cover fist with other hand)
a great big cake I see! (open out hands as if holding a big cake)
Now let's count the cakes we made – one, two, three! (repeat the size actions)

Backe, backe Kuchen

This German rhyme is easy for young children to learn. Alternately slap knees and clap hands for the first four lines; then invent an action for each of the six foods mentioned and act them out as you say the rhyme.

Backe, backe Kuchen,	Bake, bake cakes,
Der Bäcker hat gerufen!	The baker has called!
Wer will gute Kuchen backen,	He who wants to bake good cakes
Der muss haben diese Sachen:	Must have these things:
Eier und Butter und Marmelade,	Eggs and butter and jam,
Milch und Mehl und Schokolade!	Milk and flour and chocolate!

Este chiquito es mi hermanito

This charming Spanish finger rhyme teaches the different members of the family. Point to each finger on the hand, beginning with the thumb, as you say each line.

Este chiquito es mi hermanito.	This tiny one is my little brother.
Esta es mi mama.	This one is my mother.
Este altito es mi papa.	This tall one is my father.
Esta es mi hermana.	This one is my sister.
Y este(a) chiquito(a) y bonito(a) soy yo!	And this little pretty/handsome one is me!

Traffic lights

Similar to 'Grandmother's footsteps' but with more action!

Learning objectives

03.2, 03.3

04.2

Aim

To practise phrases.

Vocabulary

Instructions

What to do

- Children spread out around the room.
- One player is 'it' and shouts the instructions in TL. The last person to start doing the action, or whoever does the wrong action, is out. The last player left is 'it' next time.
- The actions are:
  - red light: everyone stand still
  - green light: run around
  - crash: lie on the ground
  - bridge: bend over to make an arch
  - traffic jam: creep along slowly on hands and knees.

Cross-curriculum link

PE

Up Jenkins!

A team game that can be played with a large group.

Learning objectives

03.2, 03.3

Aim

To play a game using TL phrases, counting and names.

Vocabulary

Numbers, game-playing

Resources

- TL name badges
- Coin

What to do

- Give each child a TL name badge.
- Divide the group into two teams, which sit facing opposite each other cross-legged on the floor. The teams are blue and red.
- Blues go first: passing a coin along the row from hand to hand, keeping it hidden from the reds.
- Meanwhile the reds slowly count from one to ten (or backwards from ten to one), then shout 'Hands up!' (TL) and all the members of the blue team must raise their fists in the air.

French: *Levez les mains!*
German: *Hände oben!*
Spanish: *Manos arriba!*

- Then the reds call out, 'Hands down!' and the blues must place their hands palm down on the floor, still keeping the coin hidden.

  French: *Baissez les mains!*
  German: *Hände unten!*
  Spanish: *Manos abajo!*

- The reds confer to try to guess which member of the blue team has the coin.
- Once the decision is made, one by one each red calls out the TL name of the blue opposite them until the names of all the blues thought *not* to have the coin have been called.
- Each blue, as their name is called, must turn over their hand.
- If the coin shows up early, the blues win a point and get to hide the coin again.
- If the reds guessed correctly, they get a point and it's their turn to hide the coin.

Verb match

Keep these card strips to re-use as a 5-minute filler exercise.

Learning objectives

L3.1, L3.2, L3.3

L4.3, L4.4

L5.3

Aim

To correctly conjugate verbs, write and pronounce them.

Vocabulary

Pronouns, verbs

Resources

- A4 sheets of card
- Marker/felt pens
- Scissors

What to do

- Give each child a sheet of card, a pen and a pair of scissors.
- The children cut the card into eight equal strips.
- On one end of each strip of card, they write a TL personal pronoun (write in pencil first, then go over in pen). For personal pronouns, see Vocabulary sections on pages 266, 281 and 296.
- Ask each child to choose a different common verb.

- After each pronoun, they write the correct part of the TL verb that corresponds to that pronoun.
- The children then cut the strips in half so the pronoun is on one half and the verb conjugation on the other.
- Ask the children to mix up the card strips and swap with a partner – each child then has to correctly match up their partner's pronouns and verbs.
- Once finished, ask each pair to read the whole set of correctly matched pronoun–verb pairs to each other.

Who am I?

Another yes and no game for older children to stretch their questioning skills.

Learning objectives

O4.2, O4.4

O5.1, O5.3

Aim

To structure and ask questions correctly.

What to do

- Ask for a volunteer to come to the front of the class.
- This child must think of a famous person – it must be someone that everyone in the class will undoubtedly have heard of.
- The rest of the class must ask the 'celebrity' questions in TL to which the celebrity can only answer 'Yes' or 'No' – e.g. 'Are you a man?' 'Are you English?' 'Are you dead?' 'Are you a singer?'
- The first child to guess the identity of the celebrity takes the next turn.

Yes or no?

Actually this name is misleading – children are *not allowed* to say 'Yes' or 'No'!

Learning objectives

03.3

04.4

05.1, 05.2, 05.3

06.3, 06.4

Aim

To ask and respond to questions.

What to do

- Ask for a volunteer to come to the front of the class.
- The other children raise their hands to ask questions in TL on any topic they choose.
- The child standing at the front must reply to the questions in TL but must *not* reply 'Yes' or 'No' to any question.
- If they do so, the rest of the class call out an appropriate TL word to show that the child has lost their turn, e.g. *'Perdu!'*
- The first child to shout out the agreed TL word takes the next turn at the front of the class.

Part 3
Vocabulary lists

French

Numbers - les nombres

0	zéro	20	vingt	90	quatre-vingt-dix
1	un	21	vingt et un	91	quatre-vingt-onze
2	deux	22	vingt-deux	92	quatre-vingt-douze
3	trois	23	vingt-trois		
4	quatre			100	cent
5	cinq	30	trente	101	cent un
6	six	31	trente et un	102	cent deux
7	sept	32	trente-deux		
8	huit			200	deux cents
9	neuf	40	quarante	201	deux cent un
10	dix				
11	onze	50	cinquante	1,000	mille
12	douze				
13	treize	60	soixante	1,001	mille un
14	quatorze				
15	quinze	70	soixante-dix	2,000	deux mille
16	seize	71	soixante et onze		
17	dix-sept	72	soixante-douze	1 million	un million
18	dix-huit	73	soixante-treize		
19	dix-neuf	74	soixante-quatorze	2 million	deux millions
		80	quatre-vingts	1 billion	un milliard
		81	quatre-vingt-un		
		82	quatre-vingt-deux		

Action verbs

crawl ramper	sit down s'asseoir
dance danser	skip sautiller
gallop galoper	stand up se lever
hop sauter à cloche-pied	stop arrêter
jump sauter	walk marcher
march marcher au pas	walk on tiptoe marcher sur la pointe des pieds
run courir	

Animals - les animaux

bird l'oiseau (m.)
camel le chameau
cat le chat
cow la vache
crocodile le crocodile
dog le chien
elephant l'éléphant (m.)
fish le poisson
fox le renard
frog la grenouille
giraffe la girafe
goat la chèvre
guinea pig le cochon d'Inde

hippopotamus l'hippopotame (m.)
horse le cheval
lion le lion
monkey le singe
mouse la souris
penguin le pingouin
pig le cochon
rabbit le lapin
shark le requin
sheep le mouton
snake le serpent
tiger le tigre
tortoise la tortue

The body - le corps

The face – le visage

ear l'oreille (f.)
ears les oreilles
eye l'œil (m.)
eyes les yeux
hair les cheveux

mouth la bouche
nose le nez
teeth les dents
tooth la dent

Parts of the body

ankle la cheville
arm le bras
back le dos
bottom le derrière
chest la poitrine
finger le doigt
foot le pied
hand la main

head la tête
knee le genou
leg la jambe
neck le cou
shoulder l'épaule (f.)
stomach le ventre
toe l'orteil (m.)

In the classroom - dans la salle de classe

Classroom objects

whiteboard le tableau blanc
book le livre

notebook le carnet
paper le papier

chalk la craie	pen le stylo
clock l'horloge	pencil le crayon
crayon le crayon de couleur	ruler la règle
eraser la gomme	scissors les ciseaux

Useful classroom phrases

Be quiet! Taisez-vous!
Give me ... Donnez-moi (sing. Donne-moi)
Listen! Écoutez!
Look! Regardez!
Repeat! Répétez!
Hands up! Levez la main!
Line up! Mettez-vous en rang!
Sit down! Asseyez-vous!
Stand up! Levez-vous!
Stop! Arrêtez!
Wait! Attendez!
Good! Very good! Excellent! Bien! Très bien! Excellent!

How do you say ... in French? Comment dit-on ... en français?
I don't know Je ne sais pas
I don't understand Je ne comprends pas
Pardon? Comment?
Repeat, please Répétez, s'il vous plaît
More slowly Plus lentement
How do you spell that? Comment ça s'écrit?
What does ... mean? Que veut-dire ...?

yes oui
no non
OK d'accord
how comment
what quoi
when quand
where où
who qui
why pourquoi

Clothing - les vêtements

boots les bottes (f.)

coat le manteau

dress la robe

glasses les lunettes

gloves les gants

hat le chapeau

pyjamas le pyjama

sandals les sandales (f.)

shirt la chemise

shoes les chaussures (f.)

shorts le short

skirt la jupe

socks les chaussettes (f.)

sweater le pull

trousers le pantalon

T-shirt le tee-shirt

Colours - les couleurs

black noir

blue bleu

brown marron

green vert

grey gris

orange orange

pink rose

purple violet

red rouge

white blanc

yellow jaune

Directions - les directions

left à gauche

right à droite

straight (ahead) tout droit

up en haut

down en bas

next (to) à côté (de)

opposite en face de

(it's) near (to) (c'est) près (de)

(it's) far (from) (c'est) loin (de)

Emotions and personal characteristics

Character traits

boring ennuyeux

brave courageux

cowardly lâche

friendly sympathique/sympa

funny drôle

generous généreux

hard-working travailleur

interesting intéressant

kind gentil

lazy paresseux

loud, noisy bruyant

mean méchant

naughty vilain

patient patient

polite poli

rude malpoli

serious sérieux

shy timide

stupid stupide

unfriendly froid

weird bizarre

Moods/emotions

angry fâché
I am bored je m'ennuie
calm tranquille
confident assuré
confused désorienté
embarassed/ashamed confus

happy heureux
nervous nerveux
sad triste
scared effrayé
tired fatigué
worried inquiet

Phrases of disgust

That's disgusting! C'est dégueulasse!   I hate it! Je déteste ça!
That's disgusting! C'est dégoûtant!   I don't like it! Je n'aime pas ça!

Family - la famille

mother la mère
mum(my) maman
father le père
dad(dy) papa
parents les parents
sister la sœur
brother le frère
daughter la fille
son le fils
grandmother la grand-mère

nan/gran(ny) mamie
grandfather le grand-père
grandad papi
aunt la tante
uncle l'oncle
cousin le/la cousin(e)
stepmother la belle-mère
stepfather le beau-père
stepsister la demi-sœur
stepbrother le demi-frère

Food - la nourriture

Basic foods

bread le pain
chips les frites

pasta les pâtes
rice le riz

Dairy products – les produits laitiers

butter le beurre
cheese le fromage
cream la crème

egg l'œuf (*m*.)
milk le lait
yogurt le yaourt

Dessert – le dessert

cake le gâteau
chocolate le chocolat
cookie le biscuit
doughnut le beignet
ice cream la glace

pie, tart la tarte
jelly la gelée
pancake la crêpe
sweets les bonbons

Drinks – les boissons

beer la bière
coffee le café
coke le coca
hot chocolate le chocolat chaud
lemonade la limonade

orange juice le jus d'orange
tea le thé
water l'eau (*f.*)
wine le vin

Fruit – les fruits

apple la pomme
banana la banane
cherry la cerise
grape le raisin
lemon le citron
orange l'orange (*f.*)

peach la pêche
pear la poire
pineapple l'ananas (*m.*)
plum la prune
raspberry la framboise
strawberry la fraise

Meals – les repas

breakfast le petit déjeuner
lunch le déjeuner
dinner le dîner

Meat – la viande

bacon le lard
beef le rosbif
chicken le poulet
fish le poisson
ham le jambon
lamb l'agneau (*m.*)
hamburger le hamburger

hotdog le hot-dog
pork le porc
steak le bifteck
sausage le saucisson
shellfish les fruits de mer
snails les escargots (*m.*)

Vegetables – les légumes

bean le haricot (*m.*)
broccoli le brocoli
cabbage le chou
carrot la carotte
cauliflower le chou-fleur
cucumber le concombre

lettuce la laitue
mushroom le champignon
onion l'oignon (*m.*)
peas les petits pois
potato la pomme de terre
tomato la tomate

Game-playing

ace, king, queen, jack l'as, le roi, la dame, le valet
hearts, clubs, spades, diamonds cœur, trèfle, pique, carreau
joker le joker
to deal (cards) distribuer
bingo! loto!
true/correct vrai
false/wrong faux
heads or tails pile ou face
odd one out l'intrus
odd, even impair, pair
higher plus haut
lower plus bas
the same pareil
I've won/lost J'ai gagné/J'ai perdu
It's …'s turn C'est le tour de …
It's your/my turn C'est à toi/moi
Ready, steady, go! Prêts? 1-2-3 partez!
You're 'it' C'est toi le chat
rules les règles
to cheat tricher
to win gagner
to lose perdre

Greetings and introductions

Greetings

Hello Bonjour
Hi/bye Salut
Welcome Bienvenue
Goodbye Au revoir
See you soon À bientôt
How are you? Comment ça va?
I'm fine thank you! Ça va bien, merci!
I'm not feeling well Ça ne va pas
So-so, not bad Comme ci, comme ça
Have a good afternoon Bon après-midi
Good evening Bonsoir
Good night Bonne nuit

Please S'il vous plaît (plural, formal)
S'il te plaît (informal)
Thank you (very much) Merci (bien/beaucoup)
You're welcome De rien
It was my pleasure Je vous en prie (plural, formal)
Je t'en prie (informal)
Excuse me Excuse(z)-moi
Pardon me, I beg your pardon Pardon
I'm sorry Je suis désolé(e)

Introducing yourself

What's your name? Comment t'appelles-tu?
My name is ... Je m'appelle ...

How old are you? Quel âge as-tu?
I'm eight years old J'ai huit ans

Where do you live? Où habites-tu?
I live in London J'habite à Londres
I live in England J'habite en Angleterre

Musical instruments - les instruments de musique

cello le violoncelle	saxophone le saxophone
clarinet la clarinette	tambourine le tambourin
cymbals les cymbales	triangle le triangle
double bass la contrebasse	trombone le trombone
drum le tambour	trumpet la trompette
flute la flûte	violin le violon
guitar la guitare	xylophone le xylophone
harp la harpe	

Names - les noms

Boys – les garçons

Antoine	Dominique	Guillaume
Arnaud	Édouard	Henri
Benoît	Étienne	Jacques
Christophe	François	Jean
Claude	Gérard	Jérôme

Julien	Nicolas	Sebastien
Laurent	Olivier	Thierry
Léon	Pascal	Vincent
Louis	Philippe	Xavier
Luc	Pierre	Yves
Michel	Robert	

Girls – les filles

Amélie	Emmanuelle	Margaud
Anaïs	Françoise	Marie
Antoinette	Hélène	Marthe
Aurélie	Hortense	Monique
Cécile	Joséphine	Nicole
Colette	Laurence	Sylvie
Dorothée	Madeleine	Thérèse
Élise	Manon	Véronique
Élodie		

Occupations – les métiers

What do you do for a living? Qu'est-ce que tu fais dans la vie?

actor/actress l'acteur/l'actrice
architect l'architecte
artist l'artiste
baker le boulanger/la boulangère
builder le maçon
butcher le boucher
carpenter le charpentier
cook le chef
dentist le/la dentiste
doctor le médecin
engineer l'ingénieur
farmer le fermier

fireman le pompier
lawyer l'avocat/l'avocate
manager le gérant
mechanic le mécanicien
nurse l'infirmier/l'infirmière
photographer le/la photographe
plumber le plombier
police officer le policier
secretary le/la secrétaire
teacher le professeur
vet le vétérinaire
writer l'écrivain

In French making these words feminine is complicated so only a few examples have been given – some, like *médecin* and *professeur*, only occur in masculine form.

Personal pronouns

I je
you tu
he, it il
she, it elle

we nous
you (plural, formal) vous
they ils/elles

Prepositions

above au-dessus de
behind derrière
beside à côté de
between entre
in dans
in front of devant

near près de
next to à côté de
on sur
over au-dessus de
under sous

In the restaurant – Au restaurant

Waiter! Excusez-moi!
Give me a menu please Apportez-moi la carte s'il vous plaît
I would like ... Je voudrais ...
Cheers! Santé!
It's delicious! C'est délicieux!
The bill, please L'addition, s'il vous plaît

What would you like? Vous désirez?
Enjoy your meal Bon appétit
Ma'am, Mrs Madame
Miss Mademoiselle
Sir, Mr Monsieur

I am ... je suis
vegetarian végétarien/ne
allergic to ... allergique à ...

tip le pourboire
waiter le serveur
waitress la serveuse

Role-play settings

bank la banque	police station le commissariat
hospital l'hôpital	post office la poste
hotel l'hôtel	railway station la gare
market le marché	restaurant le restaurant
museum le musée	school l'école
park le parc	shop le magasin

Rooms of the house – les pièces

attic le grenier	hall l'èntrée
bathroom la salle de bain	house la maison
bedroom la chambre	kitchen la cuisine
cellar la cave	living room le salon
dining room la salle à manger	staircase l'escalier (m.)
downstairs en bas	study le bureau
garage le garage	toilet les toilettes
garden le jardin	upstairs en haut

Shapes – les formes

circle le cercle	pyramid la pyramide
cone le cône	rectangle le rectangle
cube le cube	square le carré
hexagon l'hexagone	triangle le triangle
oval l'ovale	

Size – la taille

(very) big (très) grand(e)	small petit(e)
enormous énorme	tiny tout(e) petit(e)

Sports – le sport

badminton le badminton	gymnastics la gymnastique
basketball le basket	horseriding l'équitation
bowling le bowling	jogging le jogging
cricket le cricket	karate le karaté
cycling le vélo	rugby le rugby
dancing la danse	skiing le ski
fishing la pêche	swimming la natation
football le football, le foot	tennis le tennis
golf le golf	

Time, date and weather

Days

today aujourd'hui
tomorrow demain
yesterday hier

Days of the week – les jours de la semaine

Monday lundi
Tuesday mardi
Wednesday mercredi
Thursday jeudi
Friday vendredi
Saturday samedi
Sunday dimanche

Months of the year – les mois de l'année

January janvier
February février
March mars
April avril
May mai
June juin
July juillet
August août
September septembre
October octobre
November novembre
December décembre

Seasons – les saisons

spring le printemps
summer l'été
autumn l'automne
winter l'hiver

Telling the time

What time is it?	Quelle heure est-il?
It's ...	Il est ...
five o'clock	cinq heures
two o'clock	deux heures
noon	midi
midnight	minuit
two o'clock in the afternoon	quatorze heures
six o'clock in the evening	dix-huit heures
five to two	deux heures moins cinq
quarter to two	deux heures moins le quart
ten past one	une heure dix
quarter past one	une heure et quart
one thirty, half past one	une heure trente, une heure et demie

Weather – le temps

What's the weather like?	Quel temps fait-il?
It is ...	Il fait ...
bad weather	mauvais
cloudy	des nuages
cold	froid
foggy	du brouillard
hot	chaud
lovely weather	beau
sunny	du soleil
windy	du vent
It's ...	Il ...
freezing	gèle
raining	pleut
snowing	neige
rainbow	l'arc-en-ciel (*m.*)

Transport - les transports

bicycle le vélo
boat le bateau
bus l'autobus
car la voiture
lorry le camion
motorbike la moto
plane l'avion
train le train

Weights and measures

a packet of un paquet de
a bottle of une bouteille de
a can, box, tin of une boîte de

centimetre le centimètre
metre le mètre
kilometre le kilomètre
gram le gramme
kilogram/kilo le kilogramme/le kilo
litre le litre

length la longueur
width la largeur
height la hauteur
weight le poids

to measure mesurer
to weigh peser

German

Numbers - die Zahlen

0	null	50	fünfzig
1	eins		
2	zwei	60	sechzig
3	drei		
4	vier	70	siebzig
5	fünf		
6	sechs	80	achtzig
7	sieben		
8	acht	90	neunzig
9	neun		
10	zehn	100	hundert
11	elf	101	hunderteins
12	zwölf	102	hundertzwei
13	dreizehn		
14	vierzehn	200	zweihundert
15	fünfzehn		
16	sechzehn	999	neunhundertneunundneunzig
17	siebzehn		
18	achtzehn	1,000	tausend
19	neunzehn	1,001	tausendeins

20	zwanzig	2,000	zweitausend
21	einundzwanzig		
22	zweiundzwanzig	9,999	neuntausendneunhundertneunundneunzig
23	dreiundzwanzig		
		1 million	eine Millionen
30	dreißig		
31	einunddreißig	2 million	zwei Million
32	zweiunddreißig		
		1 billion	eine Milliarde
40	vierzig		

Action verbs

crawl	kriechen	sit	sitzen
dance	tanzen	skip	hüpfen
gallop	galoppieren	stand up	aufstehen
hop	hopsen	stop	anhalten

jump springen
march marschieren
run laufen

walk gehen
walk on tiptoe auf Zehenspitzen gehen

Animals – die Tiere

bird der Vogel
camel das Kamel
cat die Katze
cow die Kuh
crocodile das Krokodil
dog der Hund
elephant der Elefant
fish der Fisch
fox der Fuchs
frog der Frosch
giraffe die Giraffe
goat die Ziege
guinea pig das Meerschweinchen

hippopotamus das Nilpferd
horse das Pferd
lion der Löwe
monkey der Affe
mouse die Maus
penguin der Pinguin
pig das Schwein
rabbit das Kaninchen
shark der Hai
sheep das Schaf
snake die Schlange
tiger der Tiger
tortoise die Schildkröte

The body – der Körper

The face – das Gesicht

ear das Ohr
ears die Ohren
eye das Auge
eyes die Augen
hair das Haar/die Haare (pl.)

mouth der Mund
nose die Nase
teeth die Zähne
tooth der Zahn

Parts of the body

ankle der Knöchel
arm der Arm
back der Rücken
bottom der Po
chest die Brust
finger der Finger
foot der Fusß
hand die Hand

head der Kopf
knee das Knie
leg das Bein
neck der Hals
shoulder die Schulter
stomach der Bauch
toe die Zehe

In the classroom - im Klassenzimmer

Classroom objects

whiteboard die Tafel	notebook das Heft
book das Buch	paper das Papier
chalk die Kreide	pen der Stift
clock die Uhr	pencil der Bleistift
crayon der Buntstift	ruler das Lineal
eraser der Radiergummi	scissors die Schere

Useful classroom phrases

Be quiet! Seid ruhig!

Give me ... Gebt mir ... (*sing.* Gib mir ...)

Listen! Hört zu!

Look! Schaut an!

Repeat! Noch mal!

Hands up! Meldet euch!

Line up please! Stellt euch in einer Reihe auf, bitte!

Sit down! Setzt euch!

Stand up! Steht auf!

Stop! Hört auf!

Wait! Wartet!

Good! Very good! Gut! Sehr gut!

Excellent! Prima! Wunderbar!

What's the German for ...? Was heißt ... auf Deutsch?

I don't know Ich weiß nicht

I don't understand Ich verstehe nicht

Pardon? Wie bitte?

Could you please repeat that? Noch einmal, bitte!

More slowly, please Lahgsamer bitte

How do you spell that? Wie schreibt man das?

What does ... mean? Was bedeutet/heißt ...?

yes ja

no nein

OK schon gut

how wie

what was

when wann
where wo
who wer
why warum

Clothing - die Kleidung

boots die Stiefel
coat der Mantel
dress das Kleid
glasses die Brille
gloves die Handschuhe
hat der Hut
pyjamas der Pyjama
sandals die Sandalen

shirt das Hemd
shoes die Schuhe
shorts die Shorts
skirt der Rock
socks die Socken
sweater der Pullover
trousers die Hose
T-shirt das T-Shirt

Colours - die Farben

black schwarz
blue blau
brown braun
green grün
grey grau
orange orange

pink rosa
purple lila
red rot
white weiß
yellow gelb

Directions - Wegbeschreibung

left links
right rechts
straight ahead geradeaus
up oben
down unten

next to neben
opposite gegenüber
(it's) near (to) (es ist) in der Nähe (von)
(it's) far (from) (es ist) weit (von)

Emotions and personal characteristics

Character traits

boring langweilig
brave mutig
cowardly feige
friendly freundlich
funny komisch

mean gemein
naughty frech
patient geduldig
polite höflich
rude unhöflich

generous großzügig
hard-working fleißig
interesting interessant
kind nett
lazy faul
loud, noisy laut

serious ernst
shy schüchtern
stupid dumm
unfriendly unfreundlich
weird seltsam

Moods/emotions

angry verärgert
bored gelangweilt
calm ruhig
confident selbstsicher
confused verwirrt
embarrassed/ashamed beschämt

happy glücklich
nervous nervös
sad traurig
scared ängstlich
tired müde
worried besorgt

Phrases of disgust

That's disgusting! Das ist eklig/Das ist widerlich!
Ugh! Disgusting! Pfui Teufel!
I hate it! Ich hasse es!
I don't like it! Das gefällt mir nicht!

Family - die Familie

mother die Mutter
mum Mutti
father Der Vater
dad Vati
parents die Eltern
sister die Schwester
brother der Bruder
siblings/brothers and sisters die Geschwister
daughter die Tochter
son der Sohn
grandmother die Großmutter

grandma/granny Oma
grandfather der Großvater
grandpa/gramps Opa
aunt die Tante
uncle der Onkel
cousin (f.) die Cousine
cousin (m.) der Cousin
stepmother die Stiefmutter
stepfather der Stiefvater
stepsister die Stiefschwester
stepbrother der Stiefbruder

Food - das Essen

Basic foods

bread das Brot
chips die Pommes frites

pasta die Nudeln
rice der Reis

Dairy products – Milchprodukte

butter die Butter
cheese der Käse
cream die Sahne

egg das Ei
milk die Milch
yogurt der Joghurt

Dessert – der Nachtisch

cake der Kuchen
chocolate die Schokolade
cookie das Plätzchen
doughnut der Donut
ice cream das Eis

pie, tart die Torte, der Kuchen
jelly die Götterspeise
pancake der Pfannkuchen
sweets die Süßigkeiten

Drinks – die Getränke

beer das Bier
coffee der Kaffee
coke die Coca-Cola
hot chocolate die heiße Schokolade
lemonade die Limonade

orange juice der Orangensaft
tea der Tee
water das Wasser
wine der Wein

Fruit – das Obst

apple der Apfel
banana die Banane
cherry die Kirsche
grape die Traube
lemon die Zitrone
orange die Apfelsine

peach der Pfirsich
pear die Birne
pineapple die Ananas
plum die Pflaume
raspberry die Himbeere
strawberry die Erdbeere

Meals – die Mahlzeiten

breakfast das Frühstück
lunch das Mittagessen
dinner das Abendessen

Meat – das Fleisch

bacon der Speck
beef das Rindfleisch
chicken das Hähnchen
fish der Fisch
ham der Schinken
meatball der Fleischkloß

hamburger der Hamburger
hot dog der Hot Dog
pork das Schweinefleisch
steak das Steak
sausage die Wurst

Vegetables – das Gemüse

bean die Bohne	lettuce der Kopfsalat
broccoli der Broccoli	mushroom der Pilz
cabbage der Kohl	onion die Zwiebel
carrot die Möhre	peas die Erbsen
cauliflower der Blumenkohl	potato die Kartoffel
cucumber die Gurke	tomato die Tomate

Game-playing

ace, king, queen, jack, das As, der König, die Königin, der Bube
hearts, clubs, spades, diamonds das Herz, das Kreuz, das Pik, das Karo
joker der Joker
to deal (cards) ausgeben
bingo! Bingo!
true/correct richtig
false/wrong falsch
heads or tails Kopf oder Zahl
odd one out fünftes Rad am Wagen
odd, even ungerade, gerade
higher höher
lower niedriger
the same gleich
I've won/lost Ich habe gewonnen/verloren
It's ...'s turn ... ist dran
It's your/my turn Ich bin/Du bist dran
Ready, steady, go! Achtung, fertig, los!
You're 'it' Abgemacht
rules die Spielregeln
to cheat betrügen
to win gewinnen
to lose verlieren

Greetings and introductions

Greetings

Hello/Hi Guten Tag/Tag
Welcome Willkommen
Goodbye Auf Wiedersehen
Bye! See you later (casual) Tschüss!
How are you? Wie geht's?
Very well thank you Mir geht's gut danke

Not so well Nicht so gut
Okay/So-so Es geht
Good morning/Morning! Guten Morgen/Morgen!
Good afternoon Guten Nachmittag
Good evening Guten Abend
Good night Gute Nacht

Please Bitte
Thank you (very much) Danke (vielen Dank)
You're welcome Bitte (schön)
Excuse me, sorry Entschuldigung!
I'm sorry Es tut mir leid

Introducing yourself

What's your name? Wie heißt du ?
My name is ... Ich heiße ...

How old are you? Wie alt bist du?
I am ... years old Ich bin ... Jahre alt

Where do you live? Wo wohnst du?
I live in London/England Ich wohne in London/England

Musical instruments - Musikinstrumente

cello das Cello
clarinet die Klarinette
cymbals das Becken
double bass der Kontrabass
drum die Trommel
flute die Querflöte
guitar die Gitarre
harp die Harfe

saxophone das Saxofon
tambourine das Tamburin
triangle der Triangel
trombone die Posaune
trumpet die Trompete
violin die Geige
xylophone das Xylofon

Names - die Namen

Boys – die Jungen

Andreas	Hans	Otto
Bernd	Johann	Reinhard
Dieter	Klaus	Timo
Franz	Ludwig	Wilhelm

Girls – die Mädchen

Anke	Gisela	Lotte
Birgit	Helga	Martha
Claudia	Ilke	Olga
Elke	Katja	Sabine

Occupations – die Berufe

What do you do for a living? Was bist du von Beruf?

actor/actress der Schauspieler/die Schauspielerin
architect der Architekt
artist der Künstler
baker der Bäcker
builder der Bauunternehmer
butcher der Metzger
carpenter der Tischler
cook, chef der Koch/die Köchin
dentist der Zahnarzt/die Zahnärztin
doctor der Arzt/die Ärztin
engineer der Ingenieur
farmer der Bauer/die Bäuerin
fireman der Feuerwehrmann
lawyer der Rechtsanwalt/die Rechtsanwältin
manager der Geschäftsführer
mechanic der Mechaniker
nurse der Krankenpfleger/die Krankenschwester
photographer der Fotograf
plumber der Klempner
police officer der Polizist
secretary der Sekretär/die Sekretärin
teacher der Lehrer
vet der Tierarzt/die Tierärztin
writer der Schriftsteller

Feminine forms are usually made by adding *–in* to the end of the masculine form, and changing the article to *die*.

Personal pronouns

I ich	he er
you du	she sie
you (formal) Sie	it es

we wir	you (plural formal) Sie
you (plural informal) ihr	they sie

Prepositions

above über	near nah
behind hinter	next to neben
beside bei	on auf
between zwischen	over über
in in	under unter
in front of vor	

In the restaurant - im Restaurant

Waiter! Entschuldigung!
A menu, please! Eine Speisekarte, bitte!
I would like ... Ich möchte ...
Cheers! Prost!
It tastes (very) good! Es schmeckt (sehr) gut!
The bill, please Zahlen, bitte/Die Rechnung, bitte

What would you like? Was möchten Sie?
Enjoy your meal Guten Appetit
Mrs Frau
Miss Fräulein
Mr Herr

I am ...	Ich bin ...
vegetarian	Vegetarier (in)
allergic to ...	allergisch gegen ...

tip das Trinkgeld
waiter der Kellner
waitress die Kellnerin

Role-play settings

bank die Bank	police station das Polizeirevier
hospital das Krankenhaus	post office die Post
hotel das Hotel	railway station der Bahnhof
market der Markt	restaurant das Restaurant
museum das Museum	school die Schule
park der Park	shop das Geschäft

Rooms of the house - die Zimmer

attic der Dachboden	hall der Hausflur
bathroom das Badezimmer	house das Haus
bedroom das Schlafzimmer	kitchen die Küche
cellar der Keller	living room das Wohnzimmer
dining room das Esszimmer	staircase die Treppe
downstairs unten	study das Arbeitszimmer
garage die Garage	toilet die Toilette
garden der Garten	upstairs oben

Shapes - die Formen

circle der Kreis	pyramid die Pyramide
cone der Kegel	rectangle das Rechteck
cube der Würfel	square das Quadrat
hexagon das Sechseck	triangle das Dreieck
oval das Oval	

Size - die Größe

(very) big (sehr) groß	small klein
enormous riesig	tiny winzig

Sports - der Sport

badminton das Badminton	gymnastics die Gymnastik, das Turnen
basketball der Basketball	horseriding das Reiten
bowling das Kegeln	jogging das Jogging
cricket das Kricket	karate das Karate
cycling der Radsport	rugby das Rugby
dancing das Tanzen	skiing das Skilaufen

fishing das Angeln   swimming das Schwimmen
football der Fußball   tennis das Tennis
golf das Golf

Time, date and weather

Days

today heute
tomorrow morgen
yesterday gestern

Days of the week – die Wochentage

Monday Montag
Tuesday Dienstag
Wednesday Mittwoch
Thursday Donnerstag
Friday Freitag
Saturday Samstag
Sunday Sonntag

Months of the year – die Monate des Jahres

January Januar
February Februar
March März
April April
May Mai
June Juni
July Juli
August August
September September
October Oktober
November November
December Dezember

Seasons – die Jahreszeiten

spring der Frühling
summer der Sommer
autumn der Herbst
winter der Winter

Telling the time

What time is it?	Wieviel Uhr ist es?
It's ...	Es ist ...
five o'clock	fünf Uhr
one o'clock	ein Uhr
half past *seven*	halb *acht*
ten past two, two ten	zehn nach zwei
quarter past nine	Viertel nach neun
quarter to nine	Viertel vor neun
ten to eleven, ten fifty	zehn vor elf
two o'clock in the afternoon	vierzehn Uhr
midnight	Mitternacht
midday	Mittag
22.09	zweiundzwanzig Uhr neun

Weather – das Wetter

What's the weather like?	Wie ist das Wetter?
It is ...	Es ist ...
bad weather	schlechtes Wetter
cloudy	bewölkt
cold	kalt
foggy	neblig
hot	warm
lovely weather	schön
sunny	sonnig
windy	windig
It's ...	Es ...
freezing	ist eisig
raining	regnet
snowing	schneit
rainbow	der Regenbogen

Transport - Transportmittel

bicycle das Fahrrad
boat das Boot
bus der Autobus
car das Auto
lorry der Lastwagen
motorcycle das Motorrad
plane das Flugzeug
train der Zug

Weights and measures

a packet of ein Päckchen ...
a bottle of eine Flasche ...
a box of eine Schachtel ...
a tin/can of eine Dose ...

centimetre der Zentimeter
metre der Meter
kilometre der Kilometer
gram das Gramm
kilogram das Kilo
litre der Liter

length die Länge
width die Breite
height die Höhe
weight das Gewicht

to measure messen
to weigh wiegen

Spanish

Numbers – los números

0	cero	26	veintiséis	200	doscientos
1	uno	27	veintisiete	201	doscientos uno
2	dos	28	veintiocho		
3	tres	29	veintinueve	300	trescientos
4	cuatro				
5	cinco	30	treinta	400	cuatrocientos
6	seis	31	treinta y uno		
7	siete	32	treinta y dos	500	quinientos
8	ocho	33	treinta y tres		
9	nueve			600	seiscientos
10	diez	40	cuarenta		
11	once	41	cuarenta y uno	700	setecientos
12	doce				
13	trece	50	cincuenta	800	ochocientos
14	catorce				
15	quince	60	sesenta	900	novecientos
16	dieciséis				
17	diecisiete	70	setenta	1,000	mil
18	dieciocho			1,001	mil uno
19	diecinueve	80	ochenta		
				2,000	dos mil
20	veinte	90	noventa		
21	veintiuno			1 million	un millón
22	veintidós	100	cien		
23	veintitrés	101	ciento uno	2 million	dos millónes
24	veinticuatro	102	ciento dos		
25	veinticinco			1 billion	un billón

Action verbs

crawl	gatear	sit	sentarse
dance	bailar	skip	brincar
gallop	galopar	stand up	levantarse
hop	dar saltos	stop	parar
jump	saltar	walk	caminar
march	marchar	walk on tiptoe	andar de puntillas
run	correr		

Animals - los animales

bird el pájaro	hippopotamus el hipopótamo
camel el camello	horse el caballo
cat el gato	lion el león
cow la vaca	monkey el mono
crocodile el cocodrilo	mouse el ratón
dog el perro	penguin el pingüino
elephant el elefante	pig el cerdo
fish el pez	rabbit el conejo
fox el zorro	shark el tiburón
frog la rana	sheep la oveja
giraffe la jirafa	snake la serpiente
goat la cabra	tiger el tigre
guinea pig la cobaya	tortoise la tortuga

The body - el cuerpo

The face – la cara

ear el oído, la oreja	mouth la boca
ears los oídos	nose la nariz
eye el ojo	teeth los dientes
eyes los ojos	tooth el diente
hair el pelo	

Parts of the body

ankle el tobillo	head la cabeza
arm el brazo	knee la rodilla
back la espalda	leg la pierna
bottom el trasero	neck el cuello
chest el pecho	shoulder el hombro
finger el dedo	stomach el vientre
foot el pie	toe el dedo del pie
hand la mano	

In the classroom - en la clase

Classroom objects

board la pizarra	notebook el cuaderno
book el libro	paper el papel
chalk la tiza	pen el bolígrafo

clock el reoj	pencil el lápiz
crayon el crayón	ruler la regla
eraser la goma de borrar	scissors las tijeras

Useful classroom phrases

Be quiet! ¡Callaos! ¡Silencio!
Give me ... Dadme (*sing*. Dame ...)
Listen! ¡Escuchad!
Look! ¡Mirad!
Repeat! ¡Repetid!
Hands up! ¡Levantad las manos!
Line up! ¡Haced una fila!
Sit down! ¡Sentaos!
Stand up! ¡Levantaos!
Stop! ¡Paraos!
Wait! ¡Esperad!
Good! Very good! Excellent! ¡Bien! ¡Muy bien! ¡Excelente!

How do you say ... in Spanish? ¿Cómo se dice ... en español?
I don't know No sé
I don't understand No entiendo
Pardon? ¿Cómo?
Please can you repeat Repita por favor
Please speak slowly Habla despacio por favor
How do you spell that? ¿Cómo se escribe?
What does ... mean? ¿Qué significa ...?

yes sí
no no
OK bueno
how cómo
what qué
when cuándo
where dónde
who quién
why por qué

Clothing - la ropa

boots las botas	shirt la camisa
coat el abrigo	shoes los zapatos
dress el vestido	shorts los pantalones cortos
glasses las gafas	skirt la falda
gloves los guantes	socks los calcetines
hat el sombrero	sweater el jersey
pyjamas el pijama	trousers los pantalones
sandals las sandalias	T-shirt la camiseta

Colours - las colores

black negro	pink rosado
blue azul	purple violeta
brown marrón	red rojo
green verde	white blanco
grey gris	yellow amarillo
orange naranja	

Directions - las señas

left a la izquierda	next to al lado de
right a la derecha	opposite enfrente (de)
straight ahead todo recto	(it's) near (to) (está) cerca (de)
up (hacia) arriba	(it's) far (from) (está) lejos (de)
down (hacia) abajo	

Emotions and personal characteristics

Character traits

boring aburrido	mean tacaño
brave valiente	naughty travieso
cowardly cobarde	patient paciente
friendly amigable, simpático	polite cortés
funny gracioso	rude maleducado
generous generoso	serious serio
hard-working trabajador	shy tímido
interesting interesante	stupid tonto
kind amable	unfriendly hostil, antipático
lazy perezoso, vago	weird raro, extraño
loud, noisy ruidoso	

Moods/emotions

angry enojado	happy feliz
bored aburrido	nervous nervioso
calm tranquilo	sad triste
confident seguro	scared asustado
confused confundido	tired cansado
embarrassed/ashamed turbado	worried ansioso

Phrases of disgust

That's disgusting! ¡Es repugnante!

How disgusting/revolting! ¡Qué asco!

I hate it! ¡Odio eso!

I (don't) like it (No) me gusta

Family - la familia

mother la madre	grandmother la abuela
mum(my) mamá	grandfather el abuelo
father el padre	aunt la tía
dad(dy) papá	uncle el tío
parents los padres	cousin el primo/la prima
sister la hermana	stepmother la madrasta
brother el hermano	stepfather el padrasto
daughter la hija	stepsister la hermanastra
son el hijo	stepbrother el hermanastro

Food - la comida

Basic foods

bread el pan

chips las patatas fritas

pasta la pasta

rice el arroz

Dairy products – productos lácteos

butter la mantequilla

cheese el queso

cream la nata

egg el huevo

milk la leche

yoghurt el yogur

Dessert – el postre

cake el pastel
chocolate el chocolate
cookie la galleta
doughnut la rosquilla
ice cream el helado

pie, tart la tarta
jelly la gelatina
pancake el crepe
sweets los caramelos

Drinks – las bebidas

beer la cerveza
coffee el café
coke la Coca-Cola
hot chocolate el chocolate caliente
lemonade la limonada
orange juice el jugo de naranja
tea el té
water el agua
wine el vino

Fruit – la fruta

apple la manzana
banana el plátano
cherry la cereza
grape la uva
lemon el limón
orange la naranja

peach el melocotón
pear la pera
pineapple la piña
plum la ciruela
raspberry la frambuesa
strawberry la fresa

Meals – las comidas

breakfast el desayuno
lunch la comida
dinner la cena

Meat – la carne

bacon el tocino
beef la ternera
chicken el pollo
fish el pescado
ham el jamón
meatball la albóndiga

hamburger la hamburguesa
hot dog el perrito caliente
pork el cerdo
steak el bistec de vaca
sausage la salchicha
shellfish los mariscos

Vegetables – las legumbres

bean la haba
broccoli el brócoli
cabbage el col
carrot la zanahoria
cauliflower la coliflor
cucumber el pepino

lettuce la lechuga
mushrooms los champiñones
onion la cebolla
peas los guisantes
potato la patata
tomato el tomate

Game-playing

ace, king, queen, jack el as, el rey, la reina, la sota
hearts, clubs, spades, diamonds corazones, bastos, picos, diamantes
joker el comodín
to deal (cards) repartir
bingo! ¡bingo!
true/correct verdadero
false/wrong falso
heads or tails cara o cruz
odd one out el que sobra
odd, even impar, par
higher más alto
lower más bajo
the same el mismo
I've won/lost Gané/Perdí
It's ...'s turn Es el turno de ...
It's your/my turn Te toca a ti/me toca a mí
Ready, steady, go! ¡Preparados, listos, ya!
You're 'it' Tú la llevas
rules las reglas
to cheat hacer trampa
to win ganar
to lose perder

Greetings and introductions

Greetings

Hello/hi Hola
Welcome Bienvenido/a/(s)
Goodbye Adiós
See you later Hasta luego

How are you? ¿Cómo estás?
Very well, thank you Muy bien, gracias
Not very well No muy bien
OK/So-so Más o menos
Good day, good morning Buenos días
Good afternoon, good evening Buenas tardes
Good night Buenas noches

Please Por favor
Thank you (very much) (Muchas) gracias
You're welcome De nada
Excuse me Perdone
I am sorry Lo siento

Introducing yourself
What's your name? ¿Cómo te llamas?
My name is ... Me llamo ...

How old are you? ¿Cuántos años tienes?
I am ... years old Tengo ... años

Where do you live? ¿Dónde vives?
I live in Cervantes Street Vivo en la Calle Cervantes
I live in England Vivo en Inglaterra

Musical instruments – los instrumentos de música

cello el violoncello
clarinet el clarinete
cymbals los platillos
double bass el contrabajo
drum el tambor
flute la flauta
guitar la guitarra
harp la arpa

saxophone el saxofón
tambourine el pandero
triangle el triángulo
trombone el trombón de varas
trumpet la trompeta
violin el violín
xylophone el xilófono

Names - los nombres

Boys – los niños

Adolfo	Arturo	José
Alejandro	Carlos	Juan
Alfonso	Diego	Manuel
Alfredo	Domingo	Miguel
Angel	Esteban	Pablo
Antonio	Fernando	Pedro
Armando	Jorge	Xavier

Girls – las niñas

Alejandra	Catalina	Francisca
Alicia	Concepción	Inés
Ana María	Consuelo	Manuela
Antonia	Daniela	Paloma
Carla	Dolores	Pilar
Carmen	Elena	Sara

Occupations - las profesiones

What do you do for a living? ¿A qué te dedicas?

actor/actress el actor/la actriz
architect el arquitecto
artist el artista
baker el panadero
builder el albañil
butcher el carnicero
carpenter el carpintero
cook el cocinero
dentist el dentista
doctor el médico
engineer el ingeniero
farmer el granjero

fireman el bombero
lawyer el abogado
manager el director
mechanic el mecánico
nurse el enfermero
photographer el fotógrafo
plumber el fontanero
police officer el policía
secretary el secretario
teacher el profesor
vet el veterinario
writer el escritor

In general, feminine forms are made by changing the final o to a, or by adding a (the article also changes from el to la).

Personal pronouns

I yo
you (informal) tú
you (formal) usted
he él
she ella

we nosotros/as
you (informal plural) vosotros/as
you (formal plural) ustedes
they ellos/ellas

Prepositions

above arriba de
behind detrás de
beside al lado de
between entre
in en
in front of delante de
near cerca de
next to junto a
on sobre
over encima de
under debajo de

In the restaurant – al restaurante

Waiter! Camarero!
I would like to see the menu, please El menú, por favor
I would like ... Me gustaría ...
Cheers! ¡Salud!
It tastes good! ¡Está rico!
Could I have the bill, please La cuenta, por favor

What would you like? ¿Qué desea?
Enjoy your meal Buen provecho
Madam Señora
Miss Señorita
Sir Señor

I am ...	Soy ...
vegetarian	vegetariano/a
allergic to ...	alérgico/a a ...

tip la propina
waiter el camarero
waitress la camarera

Role-play settings

bank el banco	police station la comisaría de policía
hospital el hospital	post office la oficina de correos
hotel el hotel	railway station la estación
market el mercado	restaurant el restaurante
museum el museo	school la escuela
park el parque	shop la tienda

Rooms of the house - los cuartos

attic el desván	hall el pasillo
bathroom el cuarto de baño	house la casa
bedroom el dormitorio	kitchen la cocina
cellar el sótano	living room el salón
dining room el comedor	staircase las escaleras
downstairs abajo	study el despacho
garage el garaje	toilet el servicio
garden el jardín	upstairs arriba

Shapes - las formas

circle el círculo	pyramid la pirámide
cone el cono	rectangle el rectángulo
cube el cubo	square el cuadrado
hexagon el hexágono	triangle el triángulo
oval el óvalo	

Size - el tamaño

(very) big (muy) grande
enormous enorme
small pequeño
tiny diminuto

Sports - los deportes

badminton el bádminton
basketball el baloncesto
bowling el deporte de bochas
cricket el críquet
cycling el ciclismo
dancing el baile
fishing la pesca
football el fútbol
golf el golf

gymnastics la gimnasia
horseriding la equitación
jogging el correr
karate el karate
rugby el rugby
skiing el esquí
swimming la natación
tennis el tenis

Time, date and weather

Days

today hoy
tomorrow mañana
yesterday ayer

Days of the week – los días de la semana

Monday lunes
Tuesday martes
Wednesday miércoles
Thursday jueves
Friday viernes
Saturday sábado
Sunday domingo

Months of the year – los meses del año

January enero
February febrero
March marzo
April abril
May mayo
June junio

July julio
August agosto
September septiembre
October octubre
November noviembre
December diciembre

Seasons – las estaciones

spring la primavera
summer el verano

autumn el otoño
winter el invierno

Telling the time

What time is it? ¿Qué hora es?

It is one o'clock Es la una
It is two o'clock Son las dos
It is five past six (in the morning) Son las seis y cinco (de la mañana)
It is half past one Es la una y media
It is half past four (in the afternoon) Son las cuatro y media (de la tarde)
It is quarter past one Es la una y cuarto
It is ten to one Es la una menos diez
It is twenty to ten (at night) Son las diez menos veinte (de la noche)
It is quarter to eight Son las ocho menos cuarto
It is midnight Es medianoche
It is noon Es mediodía

Weather – el tiempo

What's the weather like? ¿Qué tiempo hace?

It is ...
bad weather Hace mal tiempo
cloudy Hay nubes/Está nublado
cold Hace frío
foggy Hay niebla
freezing Hace tiempo glacial/Hiela
hot Hace calor
lovely weather Hace buen tiempo
raining Está lloviendo/Llueve
snowing Está nevando/Nieva
sunny Hace sol
windy Hace/Hay mucho viento

rainbow el arco iris

Transport - el transporte

bicycle la bicicleta
boat el barco
bus el autobús
car el coche

lorry el camión
motorcycle la motocicleta
plane el avión
train el tren

Weights and measures

a packet of un paquete de
a bottle of una botella de
a box of una caja de
a tin/can/jar of un bote de

centimetre el centímetro
metre el metro
kilometre el kilómetro
gram el gramo
kilo el kilogramo
litre el litro

length el largo
width el ancho
height la altura
weight el peso

to measure medir
to weigh pesar

Appendices

French, German and Spanish around the world

French-speaking countries

French is an official language in the following countries:

Belgium	Djibouti	Republic of Congo
Benin	France	Rwanda
Burkina-Faso	Gabon	Senegal
Burundi	Guinea	Seychelles
Cameroon	Haiti	Switzerland
Canada	Ivory Coast	Togo
Central African Republic	Luxembourg	Vanuatu
Chad	Madagascar	
Comoros	Mali	
Democratic Republic of	Monaco	
Congo	Niger	

French is also widely spoken in the following countries and regions:

Algeria, Andorra, Argentina, Brazil, Cambodia, Cape Verde, Dominica (French patois), Egypt, Greece, Grenada (French patois), Guinea-Bissau, India, Italy (Valle d'Aosta), Laos, Lebanon, Mauritania, Mauritius, Morocco, Poland, Syria, Trinidad and Tobago, Tunisia, United Kingdom (Channel Islands), United States (Louisiana, New England), Vatican City, Vietnam

German-speaking countries

German is an official language in the following countries:

Austria	Italy (Bolzano/Südtirol)	Luxembourg
Belgium	Liechtenstein	Switzerland
Germany		

German is also spoken by a significant minority in the following countries and regions:

Czech Republic, Denmark, Former Soviet Union, France (Alsace), Hungary, Kazakhstan, Namibia (former German Southwest Africa), Poland (Silesia), Romania, Slovakia

Spanish-speaking countries

Spanish is an official language in the following countries:

Argentina	Ecuador	Panama
Bolivia	El Salvador	Paraguay
Chile	Equatorial Guinea	Peru
Colombia	Guatemala	Puerto Rico
Costa Rica	Honduras	Spain
Cuba	Mexico	Uruguay
Dominican Republic	Nicaragua	Venezuela

Spanish is also widely spoken in the following countries and regions:

Andorra, Belize, Philippines, United States

World Festivals

Here are the dates of some key festivals celebrated in countries around the world where French, German and Spanish are spoken.

5 January is the *Fête des rois* (Twelfth Night) in **France**, when a special cake is baked with a coin or other small token hidden inside – whoever has the slice of cake containing the lucky coin becomes king or queen for the day and wears a toy crown.

6 January *Día de los Reyes Magos* (Festival of Kings) in **Spain** is a celebration of the Three Wise Men; men dressed as kings throw sweets from the back of a large truck to remind people of the gifts the Three Kings gave to Jesus.

7 January is the start of the *Fasching* season in **Germany** when, along with the Austrians and Swiss, everyone attends the numerous events that include carnival balls and parades leading up to a big party in the week before Ash Wednesday.

Mardi Gras or Shrove Tuesday (**February**) is a time of great celebration for many countries around the world. In **France** ten days of wild parties, concerts and street theatre are held in Nice; in **Canada** the *Carnaval de Québec* includes snow rafting, dogsled rides and ice-skating; in **Switzerland** children dress up and tease passers-by, covering them in confetti; in French Cajun-speaking parts of the **USA** rowdy revellers in fabulous costumes hold a *courir* from house to house begging the ingredients for a communal meal; in **Bolivia** everyone gets soaked by water-bombs and buckets; and in **Haiti** people crowd the streets to watch the *raras* (marching bands).

Spring festival in **Switzerland** is when people say goodbye to winter and hello to spring by burning a huge model of a snowman.

Easter in **Guatemala** is celebrated by making beautiful carpets of flower petals for the Easter street processions. In **Germany** children paint hard-boiled eggs and give them as gifts.

23 April is the feast of Sant Jordi (St George) in **Spain**. This holiday is especially celebrated in the region of Catalonia, for whom Sant Jordi is the patron saint. During the festivities the boys give roses to the girls and girls give books to the boys.

5 May or *Cinco de Mayo* is when **Mexico** celebrates the victory in 1862 of Mexican native Indians over Napoleon's army at the Battle of Puebla. On this day many traditional Mexican dishes are eaten, such as nachos, guacamole, mole and tamales.

24 June is when *Inti Raymi*, The Inca Festival of the Sun, is held in **Peru**. The festival dates back to the Inca Empire as a celebration of the Sun God. The vivid colours Peruvians wear throughout the procession make it famous as the most visually beautiful of all the Andean festivals.

24 June is also *San Juan Day* in **Puerto Rico** – a day that commemorates the birth of St John the Baptist. People go to the beach, first walk into the water, then walk out of the water backwards seven times, throw themselves on the sand for good luck, and then jump in for a swim.

6 July is the start of the unique and world-renowned Running of the Bulls Festival held each year in Pamplona, **Spain**, when bulls charge through the narrow, crowded streets of the town.

14 July marks Bastille Day in **France**, when in 1789 a large crowd broke into the Bastille prison and freed the prisoners – this was the start of the French Revolution when the people decided they no longer wanted to be ruled by the monarchy. Today, people celebrate with fireworks and Bastille Day is a public holiday

July in **France** is when the *Tour de France* takes place, the world's biggest and most gruelling cycle race. During the course of the race, the world's best cyclists pedal a fearsome 3,550 km (2,205 miles). The competitors begin in London and ride through Belgium and round most of France, ending up in Paris.

Held at the **beginning of August** The New Yam Festival is, in many **West African** regions, the most important celebration of the year, as so many depend upon the success of the yam harvest. French-speaking countries where people observe this festival include Ivory Coast, Togo, Benin and Niger.

On the **last Wednesday of every August**, Buñol, near Valencia in **Spain**, is host to *La Tomatina*, one of the world's strangest events, where locals and tourists alike gather in the town centre to throw tomatoes at each other for an hour.

Beginning on 15 September and ending on 15 October, Hispanic Heritage Month takes place across the **USA**. The date for the mass celebrations was chosen because several Latin American countries (**Mexico, Guatemala, El Salvador, Honduras, Costa Rica, Nicaragua**, and **Chile**) celebrate their independence during this time, which also includes 12 October, *Día de la Raza* or Columbus Day.

10 October is when **Cuba** celebrates the start of its fight for freedom. On this day in 1868 Carlos Manuel de Cespedes freed his slaves and proclaimed the right of all Cubans to fight for independence against Spain. On this day Cubans say: *Viva Cuba Libre!*

1 November is the *Day of the Dead* when across **Mexico** people visit the graves of their dead relatives with vases of bright flowers and have a picnic there. Many spend the night by the grave; the next day is a public holiday when people dress like skeletons and give each other sweets shaped like skulls.

1 November is the *Día del Niño* or Children's Day in **Panama**. On this day children take the place of adults; if you have worked hard throughout the year you can be a teacher at your school or even be part of the country's government for the day. Children receive presents and go to parties at home and school.

10 November in **Argentina** is Tradition Day when people celebrate the *gaucho*, or Argentine cowboy. Dressed as *gauchos* people play the guitar, sing songs called *payadas* and children celebrate at school with folk dancing, eating typical food – *empañadas* – and drinking *mate*, the national drink

5 December is St Nicholas Day in **Austria**, when lucky children receive a visit from St Nikolaus in the evening. The older children disguise themselves as angels and devils, and the young ones put their boots in front of the door – by morning they are filled with presents.

8 December in **Nicaragua** is *La Purisima* – a celebration in honour of the Virgin Mary. People go from house to house singing songs and receiving gifts of fruit, sweets and toys. This is followed by a party where the host gives out mugs of hot *pinolillo* (a traditional drink), fudge and, most important of all, a single firecracker, to be let off at midnight.

12 December is *Día de Señora Guadelupe* in **Mexico**. On this day a colourful puppet show re-enacts the story of Juan Diego and the Virgin Mother. There are neighbourhood processions, dancers and fireworks. Many families set up shrines in their homes and statues of the Virgin of Guadelupe are placed in the windows. Gifts such as eggs, chickens, pigs and flowers are brought to the church.

24 December is when Christmas is celebrated in **Germany**. Children open their presents and at 6 o`clock in the evening a bell rings and everybody gathers around the tree, where they sing songs, read stories and tell poems. On 25 December people visit their families.

24 December is known as *Eguberriak–Olentzero* in the **Basque Country** of northern Spain. According to legend a giant comes down from the mountains, dirty after making coal from wood, and visits the local villages bringing presents for the children. The family gather for a special meal, sing Basque songs and play cards.

Eid-al-Adha and *Eid-al-Fitr* occur on different dates each year as Muslims observe a 13-month calendar. These festivals are celebrated in all Islamic countries, including large parts of French-speaking **West Africa** where Eid-al-Adha is known as *Tabaski*, a feast which involves the sacrifice of many animals.

Birthdays around the world

Here are a few interesting facts about how children around the world celebrate their birthday – why not adopt some of these ideas in your class and find out about other countries?

In **Mexico** children take turns to wear a blindfold and try to break a suspended papier-mâché animal, called a *piñata*, with a stick, releasing the sweets/treats hidden inside, which are then shared out among the children.

In **Germany** the house is decorated, and then the child's mother wakes up at sunrise and lights the candles on the birthday cake. There are as many candles as the years of age of the birthday person, plus one for good luck. The candles are left burning all day long. After dinner that night the birthday child blows out the candles. If all the candles are blown out in one try then the wish of the birthday person will come true. Presents are opened and the party starts.

Argentinians pull on the earlobes of the birthday boy or girl for each year of their age!

In **Canada** at birthday parties homemade birthday cakes are served, decorated with coloured sugar sprinkles. Between the layers of the cake a wrapped coin might be found. Whoever finds it is the first to get a turn at all the party games. In some parts of Canada the birthday child is ambushed and their nose is greased for good luck. The greased nose makes the child too slippery for bad luck to catch them.

In **Ecuador** children celebrate on the day of the saint they are named after. Saint's day parties are usually an afternoon tea party. The children are served raisin cake, cookies and hot chocolate.

In **Bolivia** at the age of 16 the birthday girl wears a white dress and dances the waltz with her father and the local boys.

In many parts of French-speaking **West Africa** a naming ceremony is held exactly one week after a baby is born. The new mother dresses in her most elaborate *boubou* and is treated like a queen. The baby is named, and the whole family and all their friends tuck into a feast and then dance to the sounds of *jali* musicians.

Useful links

http://french.about.com/library/begin/bl_begin_vocab.htm

An enormous bank of French vocabulary organised into topic areas; a similar section exists in the German and Spanish areas of the website.

www.enchantedlearning.com/

Excellent printables in all three languages (also Dutch, Italian, Japanese, Portuguese and Swedish) covering a wide range of topic areas. You do have to pay a small annual fee to access the whole site, but it is well worth it.

www.singdancelaugh.com/index.htm

Sells a range of teaching materials, including CDs of children's songs in French, German and Spanish.

www.standards.dfes.gov.uk/primary/publications/languages/framework/ learning_objectives

This link takes you straight to the webpage that gives a full listing of the Key Stage 2 Framework for Languages Learning Objectives on the Standards Site (Department for Children, Schools and Families).

https://www.cia.gov/library/publications/the-world-factbook/index.html

Sounds scary, but this CIA website is an exhaustive research tool, including detailed country profiles, maps and a complete set of flags of the world.

www.uni.edu/becker/French.html

A huge array of links to websites to do with all things French; you could be lost for days surfing here.

http://tell.fll.purdue.edu/JapanProj//FLClipart/Nounsfood&drink.html

A nice set of black-and-white line drawings of over 30 different foods, which can be printed off and used for all sorts of purposes.

www.kokone.com.mx/leer/traba/home.html

Over 20 Spanish tongue-twisters.

www.chalkface.com/info/useful-links/

A number of useful links to 'e-learning' sites from the Government's Curriculum Online initiative.

www.globaldimension.org.uk

Lots of help from the Department for International Development on including a global dimension in your lessons, with a superb global calendar of world events.

www.curriculumonline.gov.uk/Subjects/MFL/Subject.htm

Government-funded website of lesson plans and teaching resources.

www.abcteach.com/index.html

US website with membership option, claiming to have thousands of printable worksheets, many of them free.

www.factmonster.com/world.html

Similar content to the CIA World Factbook, but child friendly.

www.french-at-a-touch.com/index.html

Another enormous resource, whose strapline is 'Everything about the French speaking countries'.

www.lonweb.org/index.htm

Languages-on-the-web: thousands of links to related sites covering a huge array of languages, including the more obscure.

www.paroles.net/

Claims to have lyrics to more than 20,000 French songs.

www.thisisthelife.com/en

Travel site that lists 'reviews of the world's greatest experiences' and has a calendar of international festival dates.

http://members.tripod.com/spanishflashcards

Online Spanish vocabulary, flashcards and other resources.

www.geocities.com/Athens/Delphi/1794/childrensspanish.html

Some nice Spanish finger-rhymes and songs for young children.

www.nypl.org/branch/central/dlc/df/useful.html

For some reason the New York Public Library decided to create this page of useful expressions and greetings in 26 languages!

www.languagestickersonline.co.uk/acatalog/index.html

Online shop selling stickers and other reward ideas in a variety of languages.

http://greetings.aol.com/category.pd?path=62717

Has a fantastic range of online greeting cards in French, German and Spanish, including country-specific festivals like *Nikolaustag* and *14 juillet* (also has French Canadian, Japanese and Dutch sections).

www.songsforteaching.com/index.html

Houses the lyrics of lots of children's songs in French, German and Spanish, usefully categorised into vocabulary groups (animals, numbers, etc.) – you can also listen to the songs, order CDs or download.

www.lajolieronde.co.uk

Has an online shop selling CDs of French and Spanish songs/rhymes as well as other teaching resources.

Index of activities

Index of activities

Name of activity	Page number	'Quiet' activity	Physical activity/ requires space
Action verbs	58		✔
Actions to song	208		✔
Age walk	118		✔
Alphabet run	186		✔
Animal drawing	62	✔	
Animal matching	64	✔	
Animal mime	65		
Animal picture hop	66		✔
Animal sculptures	68		
Around ball	16		
Back-to-back drawing	155	✔	
Ball-toss counting	18		✔
Bean hunt	19		✔
Beanbags	20		
Big and small	144		
Bingo	22	✔	
Birthday dash	148		✔
Blind walk	102		✔
Blindfold body drawing	76	✔	
Body drawing	78		
Body-part count	24		✔
Body spelling	187		✔
Bubblegum	132	✔	
Call ball	25		✔
Card hunt	26		✔
Categories	156	✔	
Changing object mime	157	✔	
Character card score	104		✔
Charades	158		
Chinese relay	160		✔
Chinese whispers	161	✔	

Warm-up	Younger|Older children	Learning objectives
	O	O3.2, O3.3, L3.1, O4.2, L4.3
	O	O3.1, O3.2, L3.1, L3.2, O4.2, O4.3, L4.2, L5.1, O6.1, O6.2, O6.3, L6.2
		O3.2, O3.4, O4.2
✓	O	O3.3, L3.1, L3.2
	Y	O3.2, O3.3, L3.3, O4.2
	Y	O3.3, O3.4, O4.2
✓		O3.3, O4.2
		O3.2, O3.3, O4.2
		O3.2, O3.3, O3.4, O4.2
✓		O3.2, O3.3, O4.2, O4.3
✓		O3.2, O3.3, O4.2
✓		O3.2, O3.3, O4.2
		O3.3
		O3.3, L4.3
	Y	O3.1, O3.2, O3.3
		O3.2, O4.2
✓		O3.2, O3.3, O4.2
		O3.2, O3.3, O3.4, O4.2, O5.3
		O3.3, O3.4, O4.2
	Y	L3.3, L4.4
✓		O3.2, O3.4, O4.2
✓	O	O3.2, O3.3, L3.1, L3.3, O4.2
✓	O	O3.1, O3.3, O5.2
✓		O3.2, IU3.3, O3.3
		O3.3, O4.4
	Y	O3.2, O3.3, O4.2
✓	O	O3.2, O3.3, O4.2, O5.1
	O	O3.2, O3.3, L3.1, O4.4, L4.3, O5.1, O6.4
	O	O3.2, O3.3, O4.2, O4.3
		O3.2, O3.3, O4.2, O4.3, O5.1
✓		O3.2, O3.3, O3.4, L3.1, L3.2, L3.3, O4.2, O4.3, L4.3, L4.4

Name of activity	Page number	'Quiet' activity	Physical activity/ requires space
Grenouille	164		
Guess how many	39	✔	
Guess the sound	192		
Hand-clap circle	41		
Hangman	193	✔	
Happy families	224	✔	
Hide and seek	226		✔
Higher or lower	227	✔	
Hopscotch	42		✔
Hurry, waiter!	166		✔
I only speak ...	228		
I spy	194	✔	
Identity parade	122		
Imaginary name volleyball	135		✔
In the bag	195	✔	
It wasn't me!	136		
Japanese hopscotch	44		✔
Jumbled earth	98		
Keepy-uppy	45		✔
Knots and tangles	81		✔
Ladders	47		✔
Let's cook!	230		
Let's march!	60		✔
Magazine scavenger hunt	92	✔	
Make your own flashcards	196	✔	
Make your own jigsaw	197	✔	
Mega machine	168		✔
Memory tray	170	✔	
Multiple-choice quiz	232	✔	
Multiple-counting	49	✔	
Musical emotions	110		
Musical fingers	172		
Musical greetings	124		✔
My grandmother went to market	114	✔	

Warm-up	Younger|Older children	Learning objectives
✔		O3.2, O3.3, O4.2, O5.1, O5.3
✔		O3.2, O3.3
		O3.2, O3.3, L4.3, L4.4
✔		O3.2, O3.3, O4.2
	O	O3.2, L3.1, L3.2, L3.3, L4.4
		O3.2, O3.3, O4.2
✔		O3.2, O3.3
✔		O3.2, O3.3
		O3.2, O3.3
		O3.2, O3.3
✔	Y	O3.1, O3.2, O3.3, O3.4, O4.2, O4.3, O4.4
✔		O3.2, O3.3, L3.2, O4.1, O4.2
	O	O3.2, O3.3, O4.1, O4.2, O4.4
✔	O	O3.2, O3.3, IU3.3
	Y	O3.2, O3.3, L3.2
✔		O3.2, O3.3, IU3.3, O4.1
		O3.2, O3.3
	O	L3.1, L3.2, IU3.2, L4.3
✔		O3.2, O3.3
✔		O3.2, O3.3, O4.2
		O3.2, O3.3, O4.2
		L3.1, IU3.2, L4.1, L4.2, IU4.1, IU4.2, L5.1, IU5.2
✔		O3.2, O3.3, O4.2, O4.3
		O3.2, O3.4, O4.2
		L3.1, L3.3, L4.3
		L3.1, L3.3, L4.3
✔		O3.2, O3.3, L3.2, O4.3, L4.3
		O3.2, O3.3
	O	IU3.2, IU3.3, L4.4, IU4.1, IU4.2, L5.2, L5.3, IU5.2, IU5.3, L6.4, IU6.2, IU6.3
✔	Y	O3.2, O3.4, O4.2
✔		O3.2, O3.3, O4.2
✔		O3.2, O3.3
✔		O3.2, O3.3, O3.4, O4.2, O4.4
✔		O3.2, O3.3, O4.1

Warm-up	Younger/Older children	Learning objectives
✔		O3.2, O3.3, O3.4, IU3.3, O4.2
		O3.2, O3.3
✔		O3.2, O3.3, O4.2
		O3.1, O3.3, O4.1, O4.2
✔		O3.3, O3.3
		O3.3, O3.4, O5.1
✔	Y	O3.2, O3.4, O4.2
		O3.2, O3.3, O4.2
✔		O3.2, O3.3, O4.2, O4.4
		O3.2, O3.3, IU3.3, O4.2
		O3.2, O3.3, O4.2, L4.1
		O3.2, O3.3, O3.4, O4.2
✔	O	O3.2, O3.3, O4.2
✔		O3.2, O3.3, O4.2
✔	Y	O3.2, O3.3, O4.2
	O	O4.1, O4.2, L4.1, L4.2, L4.3, L4.4, L5.2, L5.3
		O3.3, O4.1, L4.1, O5.1, O6.2, O6.4
		O3.2, O3.3, O4.1, O4.2
		O3.1, L3.1, L3.2, L4.3
		L3.1, L3.3, L4.4, L5.3
		L3.3, L4.4, L5.3
		O3.2, O3.3, O4.2
✔		O3.2, O3.3
		O3.2, O3.3, L3.3, O4.1, O4.2, L4.4, O5.1, O6.2
		O3.3, O4.1
✔		O3.2, O3.3, O3.4, O4.2
✔		O3.1, O3.2, L3.1, L3.2, O4.1, O4.3, L4.1, L4.2, L4.3, O5.3, L5.1, O6.1, O6.2, L6.2, L6.3
		O3.3, L3.3, L4.4, L5.2, L5.3, L6.4
	O	O3.2, O3.3, L3.1, L3.2, L3.3, O4.2, O4.3, L4.2, L4.3
		O3.1, O3.2, O3.3, O3.4, O4.2, O4.4
	O	O5.1, O5.3, O6.1, O6.2, O6.3, O6.4
		O3.2, O3.3, O3.4, IU3.3, O4.2, O4.4, IU4.2, O5.1

Name of activity	Page number	'Quiet' activity	Physical activity/ requires space
Suitcase game	86		
Tongue-twisters	204	✔	
Touching encounters	182	✔	
Touchy-feely	183	✔	
Traffic lights	246		✔
Up Jenkins!	247		✔
Verb match	249	✔	
Visiting the zoo	74		✔
Warm-up verbs	61		✔
Weather guess	151		
What time is it?	152		✔
What's my line?	142	✔	
Where do you live? 1	128		
Where do you live? 2	130		
Which room are we in?	134		
Whisper, normal, shout	184		
Who am I?	251	✔	
Word chain	206		
Yes or no?	252	✔	